CONGRESSIONAL POLICIES, PRACTICES AND PROCEDURES

BIENNIAL BUDGETING

OPTIONS AND CONSIDERATIONS FOR CONGRESS AND THE FEDERAL GOVERNMENT

Congressional Policies, Practices and Procedures

Additional books in this series can be found on Nova's website under the Series tab.

Additional e-books in this series can be found on Nova's website under the e-book tab.

CONGRESSIONAL POLICIES, PRACTICES AND PROCEDURES

BIENNIAL BUDGETING

OPTIONS AND CONSIDERATIONS FOR CONGRESS AND THE FEDERAL GOVERNMENT

CAROLYN DOUGLAS
EDITOR

nova publishers
New York

Library of Congress Cataloging-in-Publication Data

ISBN: 978-1-63482-673-0

Published by Nova Science Publishers, Inc. † New York

CONTENTS

PREFACE

Biennial budgeting is a concept that may involve several variations, including two-year budget resolutions, two-year appropriations, and other changes in the timing of legislation related to revenue or spending. Biennial budgeting proposals may focus on enacting budgetary legislation for either a two-year period or two succeeding one-year periods in a single measure. This book discusses options, issues and previous Congressional action in biennial budgeting. The book provides background information on the annual character of the current process and a history of proposals to convert to multiyear budgeting; describes three bills that reflect different approaches to biennial budgeting; analyzes the potential effects of converting from annual to biennial budgeting; discusses the federal budget process; and examines challenges and proposals for adopting a long-term budget focus.

Chapter 1 - Difficulties in the timely enactment of budgetary legislation have long fueled interest in ways to structure the congressional budget process to ease time constraints. One long-discussed reform proposal would attempt to remedy this by changing the budget cycle from one to two years.

Biennial budgeting is a concept that may involve several variations, including two-year budget resolutions, two-year appropriations, and other changes in the timing of legislation related to revenue or spending. Biennial budgeting proposals may focus on enacting budgetary legislation for either a two-year period or two succeeding one-year periods in a single measure. The overall time frame for a biennial budget cycle has previously taken either a "stretch" approach, where the current budget process timetable is extended to two full years, or a split sessions approach, where all budgetary activity is expected to occur in a single year or session of Congress (typically the first), while the other year or session is reserved primarily for oversight and the consideration of non-budgetary matters.

Proponents of biennial budgeting have generally advanced three arguments—that a two-year budget cycle would (1) reduce congressional workload by eliminating the need for annual review of routine matters; (2) reserve the second session of each Congress for improved congressional oversight and program review; and (3) allow better long-term planning by the agencies that spend federal funds at the federal, state, or local level.

Critics of biennial budgeting have countered by asserting that the projected benefits might not be realized. Projecting revenues and expenditures for a two-year cycle requires forecasting as much as 30 months in advance. This might result in less accurate forecasts and could require Congress to choose either allowing the President greater latitude to make budgetary adjustments in the off-years or engaging in mid-cycle corrections, which might effectively undercut any workload reduction or intended improvements in planning. Opponents have also pointed out that oversight through annual review of appropriations would be lost under a biennial budget, with no guarantee that a separate oversight session would be effective. Furthermore, they have argued that reducing the number of times that Congress considers budget matters may only raise the stakes, which heightens the possibility for conflict and increased delay.

Biennial budgeting has a long history at the state level. The trend since World War II has been for states to convert to an annual budget cycle; however, the most recent data available, from 2011, indicate that 19 states operate with a two-year cycle, and some states operate with mixed cycles that put significant portions of their budgets on a two-year cycle.

Congressional action related to biennial budgeting first occurred in 1982 with hearings on S. 2008, the Budget and Oversight Reform Act of 1981 (97th Congress). Additional action occurred with respect to biennial budgeting during the 100th, 101st, 102nd, 103rd, 104th, 105th, 106th, 107th, 108th, and 109th Congresses. None of these proposals were ultimately enacted. In the 112th Congress, the House Rules Committee Subcommittee on the Legislative and Budget Process held a hearing on H.R. 114, the Biennial Budgeting and Appropriations Act of 2011, but took no further action. In the 113th Congress, the Senate adopted an amendment (S.Amdt. 136) to the FY2014 budget resolution (S.Con.Res. 8), that created a deficit neutral reserve fund for the establishment of a biennial budget and appropriations process. Additionally, the House Budget Committee reported H.R. 1869, the Biennial Budgeting and

Enhanced Oversight Act of 2014, with an amendment (H.Rept. 113-382). No further action was taken.

Chapter 2 - Should the Congress prepare a budget every two years rather than every year, as it does now? This proposed reform, known as biennial budgeting, has received increased attention in recent years. The Congressional Budget Office (CBO) prepared this paper in response to numerous inquiries about the subject.

The paper is divided into four Sections. The first provides background information on the annual character of the current process and a history of proposals to convert to multiyear budgeting. The second Section describes three bills that reflect different approaches to biennial budgeting.

The experiences of the states and of other countries with biennial budgeting are related in the third Section. The concluding Section analyzes the potential effects of converting from annual to biennial budgeting.

Chapter 3 - Budgeting for the federal government is an enormously complex process. It entails dozens of subprocesses, countless rules and procedures, the efforts of tens of thousands of staff persons in the executive and legislative branches, millions of work hours each year, and the active participation of the President and congressional leaders, as well as other members of Congress and executive officials.

The enforcement of budgetary decisions involves a complex web of procedures that encompasses both congressional and executive actions. In the last four decades or so, these procedures have been rooted principally in two statutes—the Congressional Budget Act of 1974 and the Balanced Budget and Emergency Deficit Control Act of 1985. The 1974 act established a congressional budget process in which budget policies are enforced by Congress during the consideration of individual measures. The 1985 act embodies additional statutory enforcement procedures, substantially modified in 1990 and 1997, that have been used by the executive to enforce budget policies after the end of a congressional session. The 1997 iteration of these enforcement procedures were set aside in the latter years of their existence and effectively expired toward the end of the 107th Congress. Efforts to renew them in the 108th through 110th Congresses were not successful. In the 111th Congress, the pay-as-you-go procedures affecting direct spending and revenue legislation were restored in a modified version by the Statutory Pay-As-You-Go Act of 2010. More recently, in the 112th Congress, statutory limits on discretionary spending and a new automatic process to reduce spending were established by the Budget Control Act of 2011.

The President's budget is required by law to be submitted to Congress early in the legislative session. While the budget is only a request to Congress, the power to formulate and submit the budget is a vital tool in the President's direction of the executive branch and of national policy. The President's proposals often influence congressional revenue and spending decisions, though the extent of the influence varies from year to year and depends more on political and fiscal conditions than on the legal status of the budget.

The Congressional Budget Act of 1974 establishes the congressional budget process as the means by which Congress coordinates the various budget-related actions (such as the consideration of appropriations and revenue measures) taken by it during the course of the year. The process is centered on an annual concurrent resolution on the budget that sets aggregate budget policies and functional spending priorities for at least the next five fiscal years. Because a concurrent resolution is not a law—it cannot be signed or vetoed by the President—the budget resolution does not have statutory effect; no money can be raised or spent pursuant to it. Revenue and spending amounts set in the budget resolution establish the basis for the enforcement of congressional budget policies through points of order.

Congress implements budget resolution policies through action on individual revenue and debt- limit measures, annual appropriations acts, and direct spending legislation. In some years, Congress considers reconciliation legislation pursuant to reconciliation instructions in the budget resolution. Reconciliation legislation is used mainly to bring existing revenue and direct spending laws into conformity with budget resolution policies. Initially, reconciliation was a major tool for deficit reduction; in later years, reconciliation was used mainly to reduce revenues.

Chapter 4 - One criticism of the current budget process is that it does not encourage or require the consideration of long-term budgetary concerns. In this context, a long-term concern is one that affects the budget beyond the traditional five- or 10-year budget window as currently used in the congressional budget resolution and the President's budget.

Some components of the budget process already deal with long-term budget issues. This means that data already exist, in publicly available formats, to assist in evaluating the country's longterm fiscal health. In some instances, data evaluating the long-term outlook of certain programs are currently available, including on those programs that are generally thought of as the most challenging to deal with going forward. Long-term components of the budget process can be separated into two general categories and are currently used for two distinct purposes: long-term budgetary data used for informational purposes and rules affecting long-term outcomes that are used for enforcement purposes.

Proponents of more formal long-term budgeting have expressed concerns that the current process allows difficult long-term decisions to be avoided, hides the long-term effects of certain budgetary decisions, and does not provide incentives or tangible goals for achieving long-term deficit reduction. To address these concerns, some have recommended modifying the budget process in various ways to incorporate a long-term budgetary outlook.

Some critics of this approach, however, suggest that information already exists to make long-term evaluations possible, so that a shift to longer-term budgeting alone would not improve the ability of Congress or the President to make the decisions necessary to achieve long-term sustainability of budget policies. Further, some have argued that there are fundamental issues that make successful longer-term budgeting impractical, such as projection uncertainty, unforeseen events, and the problem of trying to bind future Congresses to specific goals.

President Obama's Commission on Fiscal Responsibility and Reform, several outside groups, and some members of Congress have released or are expected to release budget and budget process reform proposals. Many proposals contain reform options that focus on a longer-term outlook.

Five major proposals are analyzed in this report: (1) extending the time period of the current budget window to provide greater detail about fiscal challenges ahead and the long-term effects of proposed legislation; (2) employing multi-year budget controls that would require the outyears of the President's budget proposal and the congressional budget resolution to be adhered to; (3) creating annual fiscal targets that could be used either for informational purposes or to enforce specific budgetary outcomes; (4) increasing budget transparency in various ways; and (5) switching from cash-flow accounting to accrual-basis accounting to capture the effects of future entitlements in the current budget.

In: Biennial Budgeting
Editor: Carolyn Douglas

ISBN: 978-1-63482-673-0

Chapter 1

BIENNIAL BUDGETING: OPTIONS, ISSUES, AND PREVIOUS CONGRESSIONAL ACTION*

Jessica Tollestrup

SUMMARY

Difficulties in the timely enactment of budgetary legislation have long fueled interest in ways to structure the congressional budget process to ease time constraints. One long-discussed reform proposal would attempt to remedy this by changing the budget cycle from one to two years.

Biennial budgeting is a concept that may involve several variations, including two-year budget resolutions, two-year appropriations, and other changes in the timing of legislation related to revenue or spending. Biennial budgeting proposals may focus on enacting budgetary legislation for either a two-year period or two succeeding one-year periods in a single measure. The overall time frame for a biennial budget cycle has previously taken either a "stretch" approach, where the current budget process timetable is extended to two full years, or a split sessions approach, where all budgetary activity is expected to occur in a single year or session of Congress (typically the first), while the other year or session is reserved primarily for oversight and the consideration of non-budgetary matters.

* This is an edited, reformatted and augmented version of a Congressional Research Service publication R41764, prepared for Members and Committees of Congress, dated February 2, 2015.

Proponents of biennial budgeting have generally advanced three arguments—that a two-year budget cycle would (1) reduce congressional workload by eliminating the need for annual review of routine matters; (2) reserve the second session of each Congress for improved congressional oversight and program review; and (3) allow better long-term planning by the agencies that spend federal funds at the federal, state, or local level.

Critics of biennial budgeting have countered by asserting that the projected benefits might not be realized. Projecting revenues and expenditures for a two-year cycle requires forecasting as much as 30 months in advance. This might result in less accurate forecasts and could require Congress to choose either allowing the President greater latitude to make budgetary adjustments in the off-years or engaging in mid-cycle corrections, which might effectively undercut any workload reduction or intended improvements in planning. Opponents have also pointed out that oversight through annual review of appropriations would be lost under a biennial budget, with no guarantee that a separate oversight session would be effective. Furthermore, they have argued that reducing the number of times that Congress considers budget matters may only raise the stakes, which heightens the possibility for conflict and increased delay.

Biennial budgeting has a long history at the state level. The trend since World War II has been for states to convert to an annual budget cycle; however, the most recent data available, from 2011, indicate that 19 states operate with a two-year cycle, and some states operate with mixed cycles that put significant portions of their budgets on a two-year cycle.

Congressional action related to biennial budgeting first occurred in 1982 with hearings on S. 2008, the Budget and Oversight Reform Act of 1981 (97th Congress). Additional action occurred with respect to biennial budgeting during the 100th, 101st, 102nd, 103rd, 104th, 105th, 106th, 107th, 108th, and 109th Congresses. None of these proposals were ultimately enacted. In the 112th Congress, the House Rules Committee Subcommittee on the Legislative and Budget Process held a hearing on H.R. 114, the Biennial Budgeting and Appropriations Act of 2011, but took no further action. In the 113th Congress, the Senate adopted an amendment (S.Amdt. 136) to the FY2014 budget resolution (S.Con.Res. 8), that created a deficit neutral reserve fund for the establishment of a biennial budget and appropriations process. Additionally, the House Budget Committee reported H.R. 1869, the Biennial Budgeting and Enhanced Oversight Act of 2014, with an amendment (H.Rept. 113-382). No further action was taken.

INTRODUCTION

One of the main congressional concerns related to the budget process in recent years has been the amount of time it requires. The current process, which provides for consideration of various budget questions in the form of a concurrent resolution on the budget, reconciliation measures, tax measures, public debt measures, authorizations, regular appropriations, continuing appropriations, and supplemental appropriations, has been faulted as repetitive and inefficient.[1] This, in turn, has fueled interest in the idea that the congressional budget process could be better structured to promote a more efficient use of Congress's limited time.

Despite the perceived or actual permanence of much federal spending, the process of formulating, enacting, and executing the federal budget has remained characteristically annual. This annual budget cycle poses both an opportunity and a dilemma for Congress—although the annual review of spending legislation can afford Congress the opportunity to maximize its influence concerning the funding and operation of various programs and policies, many Members have expressed concern with the high percentage of the congressional workload that is devoted to budgetary matters.[2]

The annual completion of the budget cycle is dependent on the timely enactment of budgetary legislation. Consideration of certain types of budgetary legislation is often closely linked to the consideration of other types, so that delays in consideration of one measure may have an impact on the timing of all subsequent budgetary legislation. In recent years, final action occurred on appropriations measures an average of about 104 days after the start of the fiscal year on October 1 (see Table 1). The result has been frustration with the budget process and a desire to reduce the number or frequency of budget measures that need to be considered.[3]

The budget process has also been criticized as being unnecessarily repetitive, with some questions being debated in various forms several times each year. Defense policy, for example, may be debated in terms of its priority within the overall budget in the context of the budget resolution, in terms of policy in an authorization measure, and in terms of funding levels on an appropriations bill, only to have it all repeated the following year. Rather than promote efficient consideration, critics contend, this repetition has contributed to the complexity of the budget process, as well as to inefficiency and delay.[4]

Table 1. Last Regular Appropriations Act Date of Enactment, FY1996-FY2013

Fiscal Year	Public Law	Date of Enactment	Days Late
FY1996	P.L. 104-134	April 26, 1996	208
FY1997	P.L. 104-208	September 30, 1996	0
FY1998	P.L. 105-118 P.L. 105-119	November 26, 1997	57
FY1999	P.L. 105-277	October 21, 1998	21
FY2000	P.L. 106-113	November 29, 1999	60
FY2001	P.L. 106-553 P.L. 106-554	December 21, 2000	82
	P.L. 107-115		
FY2002	P.L. 107-116	January 10, 2002	102
	P.L. 107-117		
FY2003	P.L. 108-7	February 20, 2003	143
FY2004	P.L. 108-199	January 23, 2004	115
FY2005	P.L. 108-447	December 8, 2004	69
FY2006	P.L. 109-149	December 30, 2005	91
FY2007	P.L. 110-5	February 15, 2007	138
FY2008	P.L. 110-161	December 26, 2007	87
FY2009	P.L. 111-8	March 11, 2009	162
FY2010	P.L.111-118	December 19, 2009	80
FY2011	P.L. 112-10	April 15, 2011	197
FY2012	P.L. 112-74	December 23, 2011	84
FY2013	P.L. 113-6	March 26, 2013	177
FY2014	P.L. 113-76	January 17, 2014	109

Source: Compiled by CRS with data from the Legislative Information System of the U.S. Congress.

A number of possible reforms, such as automatic continuing resolutions,[5] joint budget resolutions,[6] or merging the authorization and appropriations processes, have been advanced, at least in part, in the hope that they could make the budget process operate in a more timely fashion. For example, advocates of an automatic continuing resolution have argued that it could reduce deadline pressures in the appropriations process;[7] those in favor of a joint budget resolution suggest that it would promote early agreement on budget priorities between Congress and the President;[8] and some argue that a merged authorization-appropriations process could reduce the volume of legislation that needs to be considered in any given session of Congress.[9] As a result, some see these and other proposed reforms as offering the potential to make the timely enactment of budget legislation more likely.

Another possible approach to addressing this concern is to change the budget cycle from one year to two years, also known as "biennial budgeting." Because budgeting for the federal government encompasses a number of types of measures, biennial budgeting can have several meanings. Biennial budgeting can involve two-year budget resolutions, two-year appropriations, and other changes in the timing of legislation related to revenue or spending. Typically, biennial budgeting proposals have included at least the first two aspects. Biennial budgeting proposals may focus on enacting budgetary legislation for either a two-year period or two succeeding one-year periods in a single measure. In addition, biennial budget proposals typically require that executive branch planning and performance reviews be revised so that they are based on a two-year cycle.

This report provides background on options, issues, and previous congressional action related to biennial budgeting.

TYPES OF BIENNIAL BUDGETING

Biennial budgeting as a concept has many permutations, and may include a requirement for two-year budget resolutions, two-year appropriations, and also affect the timing of consideration for other types of legislation related to revenue and spending.

The overall time frame contained in previous biennial budgeting proposals has typically taken either a "stretch" or "split sessions" approach. The stretch approach would extend the current budget process timetable to two full years.[10] Advocates of this approach often argue that it allows for less hurried and more thorough consideration of budgetary legislation. In contrast, the split sessions approach is based on the expectation that all budgetary legislation would be considered in a single year or session of Congress (typically the first), while consideration of non-budgetary matters would occur primarily in the other year or session.[11] Advocates of this approach often assert that limiting the time frame during which Congress may consider budgetary matters to every other year or session will encourage greater levels of agency and program oversight during the other.[12]

Biennial budgeting proposals have also varied with respect to the time frame for appropriations. "Biennial appropriations" may refer to all appropriations being enacted for a two-year period, all appropriations being enacted for two succeeding one-year periods in a single measure. In addition, the consideration of the 12 regular appropriations bills might occur in stages, so that some are enacted during the first year of the biennium and the others are enacted during the second year of the biennium.

Because of the variety of approaches discussed above, biennial budgeting may have different meanings for different people. This section provides an overview of the options and selected issues related to two-year budget resolutions, two-year appropriations acts, and other possible changes in the timing of other types of legislation that might be associated with biennial budgeting. It is important to note, however, that this section does not discuss all possible outcomes and there is likely to be variance in what would occur if biennial budgeting were adopted, depending on the context and framework that was implemented. Whether these implications are viewed positively or negatively depends on the observer's assessment of the probable consequences of switching to a biennial budget, as well as the normative value placed on those consequences.

Two-Year Budget Resolutions

Since the enactment of the Congressional Budget Act in 1974 (P.L. 93-344; 88 Stat. 297), the budget process has centered around the concurrent resolution on the budget, which sets aggregate budget policies and functional priorities for Congress.[13] The budget resolution is used to coordinate the various budgetary actions that are to be taken during a session of Congress. Proposals to convert the budget process to a two-year cycle have typically involved a process centered on a two-year budget resolution.

Although the budget process is characteristically annual, there are a number of aspects of the Budget Act that encourage Congress to look beyond a single fiscal year. In particular, Section 301(a) currently requires that the budget resolution include binding figures for the upcoming fiscal year, plus planning levels for at least each of the four ensuing fiscal years. In recent years, budget resolutions have often included planning levels beyond the minimum number required by the Budget Act. For example, the budget resolution for FY2004 (H.Con.Res. 95, 108th Congress) included planning levels through FY2013. The Budget Act also provides for the enforcement of the five-year totals for revenues and direct spending, and allows multi-year reconciliation instructions. In addition, the Senate's Pay-As-You-Go point of order (Section 201(a) of S.Con.Res. 21, 110th Congress, the FY2008 budget resolution) prohibits the consideration of revenue or direct spending legislation that would increase or cause an on-budget deficit over a six-year period and an 11-year period, each beginning with the current year.[14] The Cut-As-YouGo rule in the House (Rule XXI, Clause 10) also provides a point of order against the consideration of legislation that would have the net effect of increasing mandatory spending over the same two time periods.

It is possible that Congress might benefit from only needing to adopt the broad outlines of fiscal policy every two years. As Joseph White of the Brookings Institution stated in testimony before the Joint Committee on the Organization of Congress in 1993, "Annual fights about priorities between the same Congress and President do nobody any good."[15] In addition, Congress was unable to adopt a budget resolution for FY1999, FY2003, FY2005, FY2007, and FY2011 through FY2014, and has therefore had to use other means to coordinate and enforce budgetary actions in those years.[16] Based upon this recent experience, it could be argued that it is not necessary to adopt a budget resolution every year, and that a two-year budget resolution would better reflect current practice.

It is also possible, however, that budget resolutions have served a useful purpose by providing Congress with the opportunity to participate in setting fiscal policy, and that the inability to adopt a budget resolution has been a portent of further budgetary battles throughout the year, rather than an indication that there is still agreement within Congress on the policies that were adopted in the previous year. In addition, although fiscal policy can be set for two-year periods, it is potentially subject to considerable uncertainty.[17] If the adoption of a biennial budget resolution were to fully eliminate the opportunity currently provided by the budget resolution each year to either alter or confirm current policy, it might serve to further weaken the latter stages of the process.

Two-Year Appropriations

One of the significant changes that might be made by a biennial budgeting proposal would be a two-year cycle for appropriations.[18] Under the split sessions approach, all regular appropriations measures would be considered in the first year of each Congress and could be provided either for a single two-year fiscal period or for two one-year periods. In either case, Congress would not need to act on appropriations during the second year of each Congress, except for emergency and other supplemental appropriations as needed. The stretch approach would opt instead for a process that would increase the duration of the current budget cycle so that, while the appropriations process could begin in the first session of a Congress, the fiscal biennium would not begin until October 1 of the second year. This would give Congress and the President a period of 20 months, rather than the current 8 months, to negotiate appropriations details. Under such proposals, Congress would not need to act on appropriations in the off-year, except for emergency or supplemental appropriations.

Most biennial budget proposals include two-year appropriations because, supporters contend, a biennial budget resolution would not, in and of itself, present sufficient certainty for long-term planning by agencies, significant savings in congressional workload, or enough additional time for oversight.[19] If regular appropriations were to be confined to the first fiscal year of the biennium, a possible benefit might be that additional programmatic review and oversight could occur during the year in which routine appropriations had already been provided. The extent to which this benefit would translate into greater time for the consideration of non-budgetary legislation and additional oversight would be dependent on a number of factors, including the extent to which emergency and other supplemental appropriations actions were necessary in the off-year.[20]

Current practice already includes a number of the devices proposed as part of a biennial budgeting system. For example, appropriations acts can provide for both budget authority that becomes available in future fiscal years ("advance appropriations") and budget authority available for periods of longer than a single fiscal year (multi-year or "no-year" appropriations).[21] Making these practices mandatory for all programs could result in the more timely enactment of appropriations; this outcome, however, is dependent upon the type of appropriations that produce conflict and delays in the budget process.[22] If routine appropriations are the cause of delays, then it is possible that making these decisions less often would be a beneficial change. If unforeseen and contentious issues are responsible, then widening the above practices (advance appropriations, for example) to mandate their use for all programs every other year is unlikely to result in any significant improvement in the process.

One effect of either the stretch or split sessions biennial budgeting approaches would be that regular appropriations bills would be enacted only every other year. One consequence is that Congress over the years has previously attempted to limit the amount of executive branch discretion over the execution phase of the budget process by including earmarks and other types of provisos within the text or joint explanatory statement accompanying conference reports on regular appropriations bills. A decrease in the frequency of regular appropriations would appear to reduce the number of vehicles available to Congress, and thus have a direct impact on its ability to influence executive branch budget execution in this manner.

Other Types of Legislation

Biennial budget proposals also might explicitly address the timing of other types of legislation— such as authorizations of appropriations, supplemental or emergency appropriations, reconciliation, entitlements, revenue, or other non-budgetary policy measures—within a biennial budgeting time frame.

Many biennial budgeting proposals require that all types of authorizations be enacted for periods of at least two fiscal years. Under current practice, however, many authorizations of appropriations are already enacted for multi-year periods. The main exceptions to this are the Department of Defense and Intelligence authorizations of appropriations, which are considered annually, so the impact of such a requirement on other policy issues is unclear. Most proposals also divide action so that all authorizations would normally be considered in the second year of each Congress, separate from consideration of the budget resolution and regular appropriations measures. A previous concern regarding a multi-year authorization requirement is that, unless supported by biennial appropriations, they may lack the degree of certainty required to achieve the promised benefits of long-range planning.[23] One proposed benefit of multi-year authorizations is that they could be in place before the appropriations process begins, providing for smoother working relationship between authorizers and appropriators.[24]

Although the requirement for multi-year authorizations within biennial budgeting would only affect some programs, such a system could have major repercussions for those specific issue areas. For example, Congress has operated under the presumption that the Defense and Intelligence authorizations are sensitive to a variety of foreign policy issues and, consequently, that these issues need to be addressed every year. An attempt to experiment with two-year authorizations for the Department of Defense in the 1980s proved unsuccessful. This experience has sometimes been partly attributed to the fact that the experiment was not part of a comprehensive move to biennial budgeting and was not supported by two-year appropriations. Another contributing factor was that the two-year process was overtaken by other budgetary decisions. For example, the deficit reduction concerns that led to a late 1987 budget summit between Congress and President Reagan effectively required the second year of the two-year authorization to be amended extensively. Given this experience, support for two-year defense authorizations waned.[25]

The proposed division between the consideration of authorizations and appropriations for split session approaches could serve to augment the separation of money and policy decisions currently embodied in House and Senate rules. The division also could clarify the different functions that authorizations and appropriations serve, but that some Members feel have been blurred or weakened in recent decades.[26] Conversely, there might be an erosion of the separation between authorizations and appropriations. Absent an opportunity to consider authorizing legislation in the first year of a Congress, Members might feel it necessary to use appropriations bills as legislative vehicles to raise policy questions, rather than wait for the second authorization/oversight session.[27]

The extent to which supplemental or emergency appropriations might be available during various portions of the biennium depends on both the type of biennial budgeting that was enacted and the types of appropriations that would be allowed (or not explicitly prohibited) under a particular framework. Under a split session timetable, decisions on appropriations are typically confined to the first year in the biennium, with the goal being that the second year will be focused on programmatic decisions and oversight. The degree to which separation was enforced would determine the extent to which supplemental appropriations might also be confined to the first year of the biennium, or another alternative timetable. A stretch model might also limit the time frame in which appropriations decisions can be adjusted, for example, to the period after the budget resolution was adopted.[28]

Reconciliation instructions produce a type of legislation intended to bring existing revenue and spending law into conformity with the policies in the budget resolution.[29] For such legislation to be in order, reconciliation instructions must first be adopted in the budget resolution. As a result, under a biennial budget resolution, the possibility of enacting reconciliation legislation would typically only exist once every two years, unless the rules governing reconciliation contained in the Congressional Budget Act were modified to allow for such legislation under an alternative mechanism or time frame. Some observers perceive this implication as an argument against biennial budgeting.[30]

Although biennial budget proposals have not typically addressed restricting other types of legislation, such as entitlements and revenue, to a particular time frame within the biennium, some observers have suggested that this also might be preferable. For example, under a split session approach, legislation affecting revenue or spending might be limited to the first year or session of Congress when other decisions regarding budgetary legislation are made.[31]

General Arguments Favoring and Opposing Biennial Budgeting

Aside from issues concerning how particular aspects of biennial budgeting might work in practice, a number of arguments have been made for and against its overall utility. These arguments are primarily drawn from congressional hearings, analyses of biennial budgeting by governmental committees and commissions, and scholarly articles and reports issued by think tanks analyzing various budget process reform proposals. Note that some of these arguments are based upon the potential implications discussed in the previous section. While these arguments are not an exhaustive list of all reasons why biennial budgeting proposals have been supported or opposed, and their applicability is heavily dependent upon the type of biennial budgeting being considered, they are representative of the debate that has developed over the past 30 years.

Arguments Made by Proponents of Biennial Budgeting

Supporters of biennial budgeting have generally advanced three arguments—that a two-year budget cycle would (1) reduce congressional workload by eliminating the need for annual consideration of routine or repetitious matters; (2) allow Congress to reserve time to promote improved oversight and program review; and (3) allow better long-term planning by the agencies that spend federal funds at the federal, state, or local level.

Advocates have asserted that reducing the number of times that Congress must consider budget questions would reduce the percentage of congressional time consumed by the process and would allow more time for Congress to conduct agency and program oversight.[32] By effectively dividing each Congress into a budget year and an authorization/oversight year, a two-year cycle might reduce competition for Members' time and attention, and allow for more effective use of authorizations to establish policy. Congress would not have to resort to appropriating in the absence of a current authorization as often, because the authorizations would not be crowded out of the congressional schedule by appropriations questions.[33] Another anticipated benefit has been that executive branch agencies, relieved of the need to develop and defend budget proposals as frequently, could better manage federal programs.[34]

Another argument that has often been made by proponents of biennial budgeting is that it might increase certainty about the level of future funding, thus allowing better long-range planning by federal agencies and by state and local governments. The Reagan, George H. W. Bush, Clinton, and George W. Bush Administrations all have previously expressed support for biennial budgeting.[35] The 1993 report of the National Performance Review (the Gore Commission) noted, "Considerable time could be saved—and used more effectively—in both the executive and legislative branches of government if budgets and appropriations were moved to a biennial cycle."[36] The Clinton Administration's final budget submission in 2000 reiterated its support for biennial budgeting.[37] The George W. Bush Administration also included support for biennial budgeting (as well as other budget process reforms) in the President's annual budget submission to Congress. The FY2004 Budget request stated that "a biennial budget would allow lawmakers to devote more time every other year to ensuring that taxpayers' money is spent wisely and efficiently. In addition, Government agencies would receive more stable funding, which would facilitate longer range planning and improved fiscal management."[38]

Supporters have also pointed to the multi-year nature of the budget summit agreements between Congress and the President both as evidence of the efficacy of multi-year budgeting and as a major factor in recent years for promoting more efficient consideration of budgetary legislation. Notably, the 1987 agreement between Congress and the Reagan Administration, the 1990 agreement with the Bush Administration, and the 1993 and 1997 agreements with the Clinton Administration were all built around the projected future impact of a budget plan. Subsequent budget resolutions, and budget implementing legislation, generally adhered to those agreements. By institutionalizing this arrangement, advocates of biennial budgeting posit that the success of these agreements can be duplicated.[39]

Arguments Made by Opponents of Biennial Budgeting

Critics of biennial budgeting have countered with several arguments as to why some of the projected benefits might not be realized. Reducing the number of times that Congress considers budget matters, they have suggested, may only raise the stakes, and thereby heighten the possibility for conflict and increased delay.[40] In addition, enacting a budget resolution and spending legislation every other year could be effective in reducing congressional workload or aiding longer-term planning, but likely only in the second year of the cycle.[41] Even that benefit may not accrue without accurate budget projections. Making accurate projections of revenues and expenditures is always difficult. With total appropriations for FY2010 in excess of $1.9 trillion (of which mandatory spending accounted for over one-third)[42] even small errors can be significant. Projecting revenues and expenditures for a two-year cycle requires forecasting as much as 30 months in advance, rather than 18 under an annual budget cycle, and even 18-month projections have previously been inaccurate. For example, during the FY2006 appropriations cycle, when the budget projections for the upcoming fiscal year were discovered to be $1.2 billion less than what would be required to provide for veterans' health care.[43] Such issues with inaccurate forecasting, critics have argued, might be heightened by biennial budgeting and could result in providing either too much or too little money for individual programs. Some have feared that this would increase the need for revisions to the budget resolution, supplemental appropriations, or other adjustments in the off-year that would effectively undercut any intended improvements in planning.[44]

With only a limited ability to anticipate future conditions, critics have argued that a two-year cycle could require Congress to choose either to allow the President greater latitude for making budgetary adjustments in the off-years or to engage in mid-cycle corrections to a degree that would nullify any anticipated time savings or planning advantages.[45] Furthermore, they have argued that annual review of appropriations requests is an important part of oversight[46] that would be lost under a biennial budget, with no guarantee that committees would take advantage of a separate oversight session, or that oversight separate from review of funding decisions would be as effective.[47]

In addition, critics have contended that the institutional incentives for supporting two-year budgets can vary based on the expected budgetary outcome. A budget plan that would lock in an amount for the second year of a biennium would draw relatively little support from program advocates in a time of increasing budgets (because the program might receive more generous funding later), and, alternately, would draw relatively little support from program cutters in times of decreasing budgets (because the program would be somewhat insulated from possible later cuts). In other words, these critics have asserted, an action to lock in future budgetary resources would be likely to draw opposition when some decision makers believe that a "better" decision may be arrived at in the future.[48]

In response to the possibility of duplicating the success of previous long-term budget agreements, some opponents have argued that the lessons to be learned from successful executive-congressional summits are somewhat more narrow. Opponents have suggested that while these occasional summits have proved useful in the context of facilitating the following year's budget process, it would not be possible to institutionalize the process. Instead, some of these critics perceive that the political and budgetary context that brings Congress and the President to the bargaining table on a regular basis is also necessary to ensure a commitment to implementing the outcome.[49]

BIENNIAL BUDGETING IN THE STATES

Perhaps because many Representatives and Senators have government experience at the state level, state practices are often cited in deliberations on budget process reform. In particular, 19 states operate under a two-year budget cycle (see *Table 2*), and this experience has been cited by many in discussing the applicability of biennial budgeting to the federal government.

Table 2. States with Annual and Biennial Budgets (2011)

Annual Budget with Annual Legislative Sessions	Biennial Budget with Annual Legislative Sessions	Biennial Budget with Biennial Legislative Sessions
(31 states)	(15 states)	(4 States)
Alabama	Connecticut	Montana
Alaska	Hawaii	Nevada
Arizona[a]	Indiana	North Dakotad
Arkansas	Kentucky	Texas
Colorado	Maine	
California	Minnesota	
Delaware	Nebraska	
Florida	New Hampshire	

Annual Budget with Annual Legislative Sessions	Biennial Budget with Annual Legislative Sessions	Biennial Budget with Biennial Legislative Sessions
Georgia	North Carolina	
Idaho	Ohio	
Illinois	Oregon	
Iowa	Virginia	
Kansas[b]	Washington	
Louisiana	Wisconsin	
Maryland	Wyomingd	
Massachusetts		
Michigan		
Mississippi		
Missouri[c]		
New Jersey		
New Mexico		
New York		
Oklahoma		
Pennsylvania		
Rhode Island		
South Carolina		
South Dakota		
Tennessee		
Utah		
Vermont		
West Virginia		

Source: Ronald K. Snell, State Experiences with Annual and Biennial Budgeting, National Conference of State Legislatures, April 2011, p. 3.

[a] In Arizona, some small agencies are on a biennial cycle; the rest are on an annual cycle.

[b] In Kansas, 20 agencies are on a biennial cycle; the rest are on an annual cycle.

[c] In Missouri, the operating budget is on an annual basis; the capital budget is on a biennial cycle.

[d] These states enact consolidated two-year budgets; all other states with biennial budgets enact two annual budgets simultaneously.

However, the state experience does not provide any single answer concerning biennial budgeting.[50] Some states that operate under an annual cycle have significant portions of their budget enacted on a two-year cycle. For example, Missouri enacts its operating budget on an annual cycle, but its capital budget on a biennial cycle,[51] whereas Kansas budgets for some regulatory agencies two years at a time within the overall context of an annual budget. Conversely, some states with biennial cycles do a significant portion of their budgeting on an annual basis. For example, Virginia and Oregon both enact a biennial budget that is routinely amended during the session when the budget is being executed. Minnesota considers both its operating and capital budgets on two-year cycles, but in different years. As a result, supporting examples can be found both for and against adopting a two-year cycle at the federal level.[52]

One argument of opponents of a two-year cycle has been that the trend among states has been to shift from biennial to annual budget cycles, particularly in those states with larger populations. This trend, opponents have suggested, demonstrates that biennial budgeting represents a way of budgeting less applicable to modern circumstances. In support of this, they have pointed out that, while 44 states operated with biennial budget cycles in 1940, this was because most state legislatures at that time tended to meet every other year.[53] As of 2011, with the prevalence of annual sessions, 31 states use annual cycles, including 7 of the 10 most populous states.[54] However, not all states have made changes in favor of annual budgeting. At least three states (Hawaii in 1967, Nebraska in 1987, and Connecticut in 1991) have switched to biennial budgeting after extended periods in which they used an annual cycle, while several others (Indiana, Minnesota, and Wisconsin) returned to biennial cycles after brief experiments with annual budgets.

As discussed above, one of the main arguments made by opponents of biennial budgeting has been that it would inevitably lead to greater authority for the President. Again the experience at the state level is inconclusive. Both annual and biennial budget cycles have been coupled with varying degrees of executive branch discretion and authority. For example, Maine, with a biennial budget, has far stricter limits on the governor's authority to transfer funds or cut spending unilaterally than does South Dakota, with an annual budget.[55]

The natural tension between the desire for longer planning horizons and the increasing inaccuracy of budget projections when stretched over longer periods has not been solved at the state level. This is because the same basic system of funding stability and incremental budget changes that characterizes federal budgeting also operates in the state context. Few state programs are subject to sweeping changes in any given year, regardless of the budget cycle. This might suggest that both the assertions of a need for a longer budget cycle to ensure better planning and fears related to the inadequacy of long-term forecasts of budgetary needs might be overstated.

CONGRESSIONAL ACTION ON BIENNIAL BUDGETING

Almost from the time the Congressional Budget Act was enacted in 1974, budget process reform has been a topic of congressional interest and biennial budgeting has been discussed at least since the 95th Congress (1977-1978).[56] Hearings on the subject of budget process reform have often included testimony concerning biennial budgeting. In addition, on several occasions, both House and Senate committees have conducted hearings specifically on the topic of biennial budgeting.[57] Congressional interest in biennial budgeting has also been demonstrated by survey findings[58] and by the level of cosponsorship of biennial budgeting proposals.[59]

Biennial budgeting has also been considered by a number of federal committees and commissions organized to study possible procedural or structural reforms to Congress, the budget process, or both. In addition to the Gore Commission the National Economic Commission,[60] and the Study Group on Senate Practices and Procedures (also known as the Pearson-Ribicoff Commission) recommended a form of biennial budgeting.[61] In 1993, both the Senate and House members of the Joint Committee on the Organization of Congress included proposals for a two-year budget cycle in recommendations to their respective chambers (S.Rept. 103-215, vol. 1, and H.Rept. 103-413, vol. 1).

In recent years, House jurisdiction over budget process reform generally has been shared jointly by the Committee on Rules and the Committee on the Budget; both have considered the issue of biennial budgeting. In the Senate, prior to the 109th Congress, jurisdiction over the budget process was shared jointly by the Committee on Governmental Affairs and the Committee on the Budget, under a standing order of the Senate (first agreed to August 4, 1977, and discontinued as of January 2005).[62] Jurisdiction over the budget process is currently held by the Senate Budget Committee.[63]

Congressional action related to biennial budgeting first occurred in 1982 with hearings on S. 2008, the Budget and Oversight Reform Act of 1981 (97th Congress). Additional action, outlined below, occurred with respect to biennial budgeting during the 100th, 101st, 102nd, 103rd, 104th, 105th, 106th, 107th, 108th, 109th, 112th, and 113thCongresses. None of these proposals were ultimately enacted. In the 112th Congress, the House Rules Committee Subcommittee on the Legislative and Budget Process held a hearing on H.R. 114, the Biennial Budgeting and Appropriations Act of 2011; no further action occurred during that Congress. In the 113th Congress, the Senate adopted an amendment (S.Amdt. 136) to the FY2014 budget resolution

(S.Con.Res. 8) that created a deficit neutral reserve fund for the establishment of a biennial budget and appropriations process.[64] Additionally, the House Budget Committee reported H.R. 1869, the Biennial Budgeting and Enhanced Oversight Act of 2014, with an amendment (H.Rept. 113-382).

97th Congress

S. 2008, the Budget and Oversight Reform Act of 1981, was introduced on January 25, 1982. This bill would have amended the Congressional Budget Act to provide for a biennial budget cycle. The measure was jointly referred to the Senate Committee on the Budget and Committee on Governmental Affairs. The Committee on the Budget held hearings on the measure on September 14, 16, 21, and 23, 1982. S. 2008 was not reported out of committee.

100th Congress

On May 6, 1987, during consideration of S.Con.Res. 49, the budget resolution for FY1988, an amendment (S.Amdt. 186 to S.Amdt. 174) was offered on the floor of the Senate to express the sense of the Congress that biennial budget process should be enacted into law that year. The amendment was tabled, 53-45.[65]

S. 2478, the Biennial Budget Act of 1988, was introduced on June 7, 1988. The measure was jointly referred to the Senate Committee on the Budget and Committee on Governmental Affairs. The Committee on Governmental Affairs held hearings on the measure on June 7, 1988. S. 2478 was reported by the Committee on Governmental Affairs on August 25, 1988, with amendments (S.Rept. 100-499). No further action was taken.

101st Congress

S. 29, the Biennial Budget Act, was introduced on January 25, 1989. The measure was jointly referred to the Senate Committee on the Budget and Committee on Governmental Affairs. The Committees on Budget and Governmental Affairs held joint hearings on the measure on October 18, 1989. S. 29 was reported by the Committee on Governmental Affairs on March 21, 1990 (S.Rept. 101-254). No further action was taken.

On May 4, 1989, during consideration of S.Con.Res. 30, the Senate budget resolution for FY1990, an amendment (S.Amdt. 88) was offered on the floor of the Senate to express the sense of the Senate that Congress should enact legislation to establish a biennial budget process. The amendment was agreed to by a voice vote[66] and was included in the Senate substitute amendment to H.Con.Res. 106, the vehicle for the FY1990 budget resolution. This provision was ultimately removed in conference (H.Rept. 101-50).

102nd Congress

H.R. 1889, the Budget Simplification and Reform Act of 1991, was introduced on April 17, 1991. This budget process reform bill included provisions establishing a biennial budget. The measure was jointly referred to Committee on Governmental Operations (and subsequently referred to the Subcommittee on Legislation and National Security) and the Committee on Rules (and subsequently referred to the Subcommittee on the Legislative Process). The Subcommittee on the Legislative Process held hearings on the measure on September 18 and 25, 1992. H.R. 1889 was not reported out of committee.

103rd Congress

H.R. 3801, the Legislative Reorganization Act of 1994, was introduced on February 3, 1994. This bill included provisions establishing a biennial budget. The measure was jointly referred to the Committees on Government Operations, House Administration, and Rules (and subsequently referred to the Subcommittee on the Rules of the House and Subcommittee on the Legislative Process). The Committee on House Administration held hearings on the measure on June 14, 30, and July 14, 1994. The Subcommittee on the Rules of the House held hearings on March 9, 10, 16, 24, and April 13, 1994. The Subcommittee on Legislative Process held hearings on February 25 and March 2, 1994. No further action was taken.

S. 1824, the companion measure to H.R. 3801, was introduced on February 3, 1994. The measure was referred to the Committee on Rules, which held hearings on February 10, 24, March 10, 17, and April 28 (S.Hrg. 103-488). The bill was reported with an amendment on July 1, 1994 (S.Rept. 103-297).[67] No further action was taken.

105th Congress

S. 261, the Biennial Budgeting and Appropriations Act, was introduced on February 4, 1997. The measure was jointly referred to the Committee on the Budget and Committee on Governmental Affairs. The Committee on the Budget held a hearing on February 13, 1997. The Committee on Governmental Affairs held a hearing on April 23, 1997 (S.Hrg. 105-138). The bill was reported by the Committee on Governmental Affairs with an amendment in the nature of a substitute on September 4, 1997 (S.Rept. 105-72). No further action was taken.

106th Congress

S.92, the Biennial Budgeting and Appropriations Act, was introduced on January 19, 1999. The measure was jointly referred to the Committee on the Budget and Committee on Governmental Affairs. The Committees on the Budget and Governmental Affairs held a joint hearing on January 27, 1999. The bill was reported by the Committee on Governmental Affairs with an amendment in the nature of a substitute on March 10, 1999 (S.Rept. 106-12). No further action was taken.

S.93, the Budget Enforcement Act of 1999, was introduced on January 19, 1999. This bill included provisions providing for a biennial budget. The measure was jointly referred to the Committee on the Budget and Committee on Governmental Affairs. The Committees on the Budget and Governmental Affairs held a joint hearing on January 27, 1999. No further action was taken.

On May 16, 2000, during consideration of H.R. 853, an amendment (H.Amdt. 708) was offered on the floor of the House to add a new title establishing a biennial budget process. The amendment was rejected, 201-217.[68]

107th Congress

H.R. 981, the Budget Responsibility and Efficiency Act of 2001, was introduced on March 13, 2001. This bill would have amended the Congressional Budget Act to provide for a biennial budget cycle. The measure was jointly referred to the Committee on the Budget, Committee on Rules, and Committee on Government Reform. The Committee on the Budget reported the measure with an amendment on September 5, 2001 (H.Rept. 107-200, Part I). The Committee on Rules reported the measure with an amendment on November 14, 2001 (H.Rept. 107-200, Part 2). No further action was taken.

108th Congress

During House consideration of H.R. 4663, the Spending Control Act of 2004, an amendment (H.Amdt. 621) was offered that sought to replace the text of the bill with the "Family Budget Protection Act of 2004," a budget process reform proposal containing provisions to provide for a biennial budget. The amendment was rejected, 88-326.[69]

109th Congress

S. 3521, the Stop Over Spending Act of 2006, was introduced on June 15, 2006. This bill contained provisions providing for a biennial budget cycle. The measure was referred to the Committee on the Budget, which reported the measure with an amendment on July 14, 2006 (S.Rept. 109-283). No further action was taken.

112th Congress

H.R. 114, the Biennial Budgeting and Appropriations Act of 2011, was introduced on January 5, 2011. The measure was jointly referred to the Committees on the Budget, Oversight and Government Reform, and Rules (and subsequently referred to the Subcommittee on the Legislative and Budget Process). The Subcommittee on the Legislative and Budget Process held a hearing on January 24, 2012. No further action was taken.

113th Congress

During Senate consideration of S.Con.Res. 8, the FY2014 budget resolution, an amendment was offered that created a deficit neutral reserve fund for the establishment of a biennial budget and appropriations process (S.Amdt. 136).[70] The amendment was adopted, 68-31.[71] The resolution passed the Senate, 50-49, but final action on resolving differences did not occur before the end of the Congress.

H.R. 1869, the Biennial Budgeting and Enhanced Oversight Act of 2014, was introduced on May 8, 2013. The measure was jointly referred to the Committees on the Budget, Oversight and Government Reform, and Rules. The Committee on the Budget reported the measure with an amendment on March 21, 2014 (H.Rept. 113-382). After the measure was discharged from the Committee on Oversight and Government Reform on March 21, 2014, and the Committee on Rules on December 11, 2014, no further congressional action occurred.[72]

End Notes

[1] For general information on the congressional budget process, see CRS Report 98-721, Introduction to the Federal Budget Process, coordinated by Bill Heniff Jr.

[2] This workload is illustrated by the number of budget related roll call votes, as shown in Norman J. Ornstein, Thomas E. Mann, and Michael J. Malbin, Vital Statistics on Congress: 2008 (Washington: Brookings Institute Press, 2008), chap. 7, p. 141.

[3] For more on this perspective, see, Rudolph G. Penner and Alan J. Abramson, Broken Purse Strings (Washington: The Urban Institute Press, 1988), p. 110.

[4] For more on this perspective, see Prepared Statement of Senator Pete Domenici, in U.S. Congress, Senate Committee on Governmental Affairs, Subcommittee on Financial Management and Accountability, S. 1434—Biennial Budgeting Act of 1995, hearing, 104th Cong., 2nd sess., July 24, 1996, S.Hrg. 104-638 (Washington, DC: GPO, 1996).

[5] For further information on automatic continuing resolutions, see CRS Report R41948, Automatic Continuing Resolutions: Background and Overview of Recent Proposals, by Jessica Tollestrup.

[6] For further information joint budget resolutions, see CRS Report R42383, Budget Process Reform: Proposals and Legislative Actions in 2012, by Megan S. Lynch.

[7] For more on this perspective, see the testimony of Martha Phillips, Concord Coalition, U.S. Congress, Senate Committee on the Budget and Committee on Governmental Affairs, To Consider Budget Process Reform, joint hearing, 106th Cong., 1st sess., S.Hrg. 106-24 (Washington, DC: GPO 1999), p. 63; Brian M. Riedl, "Backgrounder: 10 Elements of Comprehensive Budget Process Reform," The Heritage Foundation, no. 1943, June 15, 2006, p. 7.

[8] For more on this perspective, see Penner and Abramson, Broken Purse Strings, pp. 113-114.

[9] See, for example, Testimony of Tim Roemer, in U.S. Congress, Senate Select Committee on Intelligence, Congressional Oversight of Intelligence Activities, hearing, 110th Cong., 1st sess., November 13, 2007, S.Hrg. 110-794 (Washington, DC: GPO, 2007).

[10] See, for example, S. 211 and H.R. 114 (112th Cong.).

[11] See, for example, S. 286 and H.R. 22 (100th Cong.).

[12] For a more extensive discussion of the differences between these approaches, see U.S. Congressional Budget Office, Biennial Budgeting, February 1988, pp. 1-2.

[13] For further information on the budget resolution, see CRS Report 98-512, Formulation and Content of the Budget Resolution and CRS Report 98-511, Consideration of the Budget Resolution, by Bill Heniff Jr.

[14] For more on the Senate PAYGO point of order, see CRS Report RL31943, Budget Enforcement Procedures: Senate Pay-As-You-Go (PAYGO) Rule, by Bill Heniff Jr.

[15] U.S. Congress, Joint Committee on the Organization of Congress, Budget Process: Testimony of Hon. Anthony Beilenson and a Panel of Experts, 103rd Cong., 1st sess., Mar. 23, 1993 (Washington,: GPO, 1993), p. 82.

[16] See CRS Report RL31443, The "Deeming Resolution": A Budget Enforcement Tool, by Megan S. Lynch.

[17] For a discussion of challenges related to long-term budgeting, see CRS Report R41516, Adopting a Long-Term Budget Focus: Challenges and Proposals, by Megan S. Lynch, Marc Labonte, and Mindy R. Levit.

[18] For general information on the appropriations process, see CRS Report R42388, The Congressional Appropriations Process: An Introduction, by Jessica Tollestrup.

[19] Testimony of Alice M. Rivlin, in U.S. Congress, House Committee on Government Operations, Subcommittee on Legislation and National Security, Reform of the Federal Budget Process, hearing, 100th Cong., 1st sess., March 12, April 2, and 30, H.Rept. 401-43 (Washington, DC: GPO, 1987).

[20] Observers disagree as to the extent to which off-year appropriations might be necessary within a biennial budgeting cycle. For more on this debate, see Robert Greenstein and James Horney, "Biennial Budgeting: Do the Drawbacks Outweigh the Advantages?," Center on Budget and Policy Priorities, June 16, 2006 and David Kendall and Jim Kessler, "Biennial Budgeting: Better Value for Taxpayers," Third Way, September 2010.

[21] For further information on the future provision of budget authority, see CRS Report RS20441, Advance Appropriations, Forward Funding, and Advance Funding, by Sandy Streeter.

[22] Testimony of Director, Congressional Budget Office, Dan L. Crippen, in U.S. Congress, House Committee on Rules, Biennial Budgeting: A Tool for Promoting Fiscal Management and Oversight, hearing, 106th Cong., 2nd sess., February 16, March 10 and 16, H.Hrg.106-681 (Washington, DC: GPO, 2000).

[23] For further information on the relationship of authorizations and appropriations, see CRS Report R42098, Authorization of Appropriations: Procedural and Legal Issues, by Jessica Tollestrup and Brian T. Yeh.

[24] Rep. William H. Natcher, chairman of the House Appropriations Committee, testified in 1993 that requiring multiyear authorizations to be enacted the year before appropriations measures would serve the Congress well. U.S. Congress, Joint Committee on the Organization of Congress, Budget Process: Testimony of Hon. William H. Natcher, hearing, 103rd Cong., 1st sess., March 11, 1993 (Washington: GPO, 1993), p. 5.

[25] David C. Morrison, "Two at a Time," National Journal, vol. 21, no. 35 (September 2, 1989), p. 2172; and Robert J. Art, "The Pentagon: The Case for Biennial Budgeting," Political Science Quarterly, vol. 104, no. 2 (summer 1989), pp. 193-214.

[26] As illustrated by testimony on budget process reform on several occasions in recent years. One example is the extensive testimony before the Joint Committee on the Organization of Congress in 1992.

[27] Testimony of Deputy Director, Congressional Budget Office, James L. Blum, in U.S. Congress, Senate Committee on Governmental Affairs, Subcommittee on Financial Management and Accountability, S. 1434—Biennial Budgeting Act of 1995, hearing, 104th Cong., 2nd sess., July 24, 1996, S.Hrg. 104-638 (Washington, DC: GPO, 1996).

[28] For a discussion of this possibility, see U.S. Congress, Senate Committee on Governmental Affairs, Proposed Budget Reforms: A Critical Analysis, committee print, 100th Cong., 2nd sess., April 1988, S.Prt. 100-98 (Washington: GPO, 1988), pp. 22-23.

[29] For further information on reconciliation, see CRS Report 98-814, Budget Reconciliation Legislation: Development and Consideration, by Bill Heniff Jr.

[30] See, for example, Prepared Statement of Congressman Nick Smith, in U.S. Congress, House Committee on Rules, Biennial Budgeting: A Tool for Promoting Fiscal Management and Oversight, hearing, 106th Cong., 2nd sess., February 16, March 10 and 16, H.Hrg.106-681 (Washington, DC: GPO, 2000).

[31] See, for example, Testimony of Director, Congressional Budget Office, Dan L. Crippen, in U.S. Congress, House Committee on Rules, Biennial Budgeting: A Tool for Promoting Fiscal Management and Oversight, hearing, 106th Cong., 2nd sess., February 16, March 10 and 16, H.Hrg.106-681 (Washington, DC: GPO, 2000).

[32] See, for example, Prepared Statement of Senator Pete Domenici, in U.S. Congress, Senate Committee on Governmental Affairs, Subcommittee on Financial Management and Accountability, S. 1434—Biennial Budgeting Act of 1995, hearing, 104th Cong., 2nd sess., July 24, 1996, S.Hrg. 104-638 (Washington, DC: GPO, 1996).

[33] See, for example, Prepared Statement of Senator Wendell H. Ford, in U.S. Congress, Senate Committee on Governmental Affairs, Subcommittee on Financial Management and Accountability, S. 1434—Biennial Budgeting Act of 1995, hearing, 104th Cong., 2nd sess., July 24, 1996, S.Hrg. 104-638 (Washington, DC: GPO, 1996).

[34] See, for example, U.S. Office of the Vice President, Creating a Government That Works Better and Costs Less: Mission-Driven, Results-Oriented Budgeting, accompanying report of the National Performance Review (Washington: GPO, 1993).

[35] As of the date of this report, the Obama Administration has not adopted an official position on biennial budgeting.

[36] Vice President, Creating a Government That Works Better and Costs Less: Mission-Driven, Results-Oriented Budgeting, p. 59.

[37] U.S. Office of Management and Budget, Budget of the United States Government, Fiscal Year 2001, Analytical Perspectives (Washington: GPO, 2000), p. 287.

[38] U.S. Office of Management and Budget, Budget of the United States Government, Fiscal Year 2004, Analytical Perspectives (Washington: GPO, 2003), p. 318.

[39] For a discussion of this issue, see Testimony of Associate Director, U.S. General Accounting Office, Susan J. Irving, in U.S. Congress, Senate Committee on Governmental Affairs, Subcommittee on Financial Management and Accountability, S. 1434—Biennial Budgeting Act of 1995, hearing, 104th Cong., 2nd sess., July 24, 1996, S.Hrg. 104- 638 (Washington, DC: GPO, 1996).

[40] See, for example, Louis Fisher, "Biennial Budgeting in the Federal Government," Public Budgeting and Finance, vol. 17, no. 3 (fall 1997), p. 89 and Greenstein and Horney, "Biennial Budgeting: Do the Drawbacks Outweigh the Advantages?"

[41] See, for example, Testimony of Deputy Director, Congressional Budget Office, James L. Blum, in U.S. Congress, Senate Committee on Governmental Affairs, Subcommittee on Financial Management and Accountability, S. 1434— Biennial Budgeting Act of 1995, hearing, 104th Cong., 2nd sess., July 24, 1996, S.Hrg. 104-638 (Washington, DC: GPO, 1996).

[42] U.S. Congress, House Committee on Appropriations, Report of Committee Activities, 111th Cong., 2nd sess., H.Rept. 111-700 (Washington, DC: GPO 2011), p. 5.

[43] The reason for this shortfall was attributed at that time, in part, to the unexpected rise in the number of veterans enrolling in the health care system. For further information, see Tim Starks, "Bill Targets Veteran's Funding Shortfall," CQ Weekly Report, November 21, 2005, p. 3136.

[44] Penner and Abramson, Broken Purse Strings, pp. 116-117 and Greenstein and Horney, "Biennial Budgeting: Do the Drawbacks Outweigh the Advantages?."

[45] See, for example, Fisher, "Biennial Budgeting in the Federal Government," p. 91.

[46] For a discussion of appropriations oversight, see CRS Report RL30240, Congressional Oversight Manual, by Alissa M. Dolan et al.

[47] See, for example, Testimony of Associate Director, U.S. General Accounting Office, Susan J. Irving, in U.S. Congress, Senate Committee on Governmental Affairs, Subcommittee on Financial Management and Accountability, S. 1434—Biennial Budgeting Act of 1995, hearing, 104th Cong., 2nd sess., July 24, 1996, S.Hrg. 104-638 (Washington, DC: GPO, 1996).

[48] See, for example, Testimony of Robert Greenstein, in U.S. Congress, House Committee on Rules, Biennial Budgeting: A Tool for Promoting Fiscal Management and Oversight, hearing, 106th Cong., 2nd sess., February 16, March 10 and 16, H.Hrg.106-681 (Washington, DC: GPO, 2000).

[49] Prepared statement of Congressman Porter J. Goss, in U.S. Congress, House Committee on Rules, Biennial Budgeting: A Tool for Promoting Fiscal Management and Oversight, hearing, 106th Cong., 2nd sess., February 16, March 10 and 16, H.Hrg.106-681 (Washington, DC: GPO, 2000).

[50] This has been concluded by the Government Accountability Office in a number of studies on biennial budgeting and the states. See, for example, U.S. Government Accountability Office, Biennial Budgeting: Three States' Experiences, GAO-01-132, October 2000, p. 6.

[51] An operating budgeting accounts for day-to-day government expenditures and is typically funded with current revenues such as taxes and short-term debt (less than one-year maturity). A capital budget accounts for capital expenditures that are funded by a mix of long-term debt and current revenues.

[52] Ronald K. Snell, "Annual vs. Biennial Budgeting: No Clear Winner," Spectrum, vol. 68 (winter 1995), p. 23.

[53] National Conference of State Legislatures, "Table 7-1: Executive Authority to Cut the Enacted Budget," September 2008. Available at http://www.ncsl.org/issues-research/budget/executive-authority-to-cut-the-enacted-budget.aspx.

[54] California, Florida, Georgia, Michigan, New York, and Pennsylvania all operate with annual cycles, whereas North Carolina, Ohio and Texas operate with biennial cycles.

[55] Snell, "Annual vs. Biennial Budgeting: No Clear Winner," p. 23.

[56] For a more detailed discussion of earlier consideration of biennial budgeting, see U.S. Congress, Senate Committee on Rules and Administration, Improving the Operation of the Legislative Branch of the Federal Government, and for Other Purposes, report to accompany S. 1824, 103rd Cong., 2nd sess., S.Rept. 103-297 (Washington: GPO, 1994), pp. 10-14.

[57] Printed hearings specifically addressing the issue of biennial budgeting include U.S. Congress, House Committee on Government Operations, The Vice President's National Performance Review—Recommending A Biennial Budget Process, hearings, 103rd Cong., 1st sess., October 7, 1993 (Washington: GPO, 1994); and U.S. Congress, Senate Committee on Governmental Affairs, S. 261—Biennial Budgeting and Appropriations Act, hearings, 105th Cong., 1st sess., April 23, 1997 (Washington: GPO, 1997).

[58] For example, 85% of Representatives and 87.5% of Senators responding to a 1987 survey indicated that they agreed or strongly agreed with the idea of appropriating on a two-year schedule. Congress Speaks—A Survey of the 100th Congress (Washington: Center for Responsive Politics, 1988), pp. 34.

[59] For example, H.Res. 396 (106th Congress) was introduced by Representative David Dreier on November 18, 1999 with 245 cosponsors, expressing the sense of the House in favor of biennial budgeting legislation. More recently, H.R. 1869 (113th Cong.), which would have implemented biennial budgeting, had 142 cosponsors by the end of the 113th Congress.

[60] U.S. National Economic Commission, Report of the National Economic Commission (Washington: GPO, 1989), p. 11.

[61] The Pearson-Ribicoff Commission recommended that Congress consider half of the regular appropriations bills each year. For further information, see U.S. Congress, Senate Committee on Rules and Administration, Report of the Study Group on Senate Practices and Procedures, committee print, 98th Cong., 2nd sess., S. Prt. 98-242 (Washington: GPO, 1984), p. 21.

[62] This order provided that if one committee reported a measure, the other had 30 days to report or be discharged from further consideration.

[63] This change was provided for under the terms of S.Res. 445 (108th Congress) and has continued in effect through the date of this report.

[64] For further information on reserve funds and the congressional budget resolution, see CRS Report RL33122, Congressional Budget Resolutions: Revisions and Adjustments, by Robert Keith.

[65] Senate debate, Congressional Record, vol. 133, part 9 (May 6, 1987), p. 11437.

[66] Senate debate, Congressional Record, vol. 135, part 6 (May 4, 1989), p. 8234.

[67] It is notable that in contrast to the comprehensive approach to biennial budgeting taken in most biennial budgeting proposals, S. 1824, as reported, included two-year budget resolutions and multi-year authorizations, but not two-year appropriations.

[68] House debate, Congressional Record, vol. 146, part 6 (May 16, 2000), p. 7978.

[69] House debate, Congressional Record, vol. 150, part 10 (June 24, 2004), p. 14089.

[70] For further information on reserve funds and the congressional budget resolution, see CRS Report RL33122, Congressional Budget Resolutions: Revisions and Adjustments, by Robert Keith.

[71] Senate debate, Congressional Record, daily edition, vol. 159, part 43 (March 22, 2013), p. S2282.

[72] Other legislation that included biennial budgeting proposals was introduced in the 113th Congress. This legislation included H.R. 879, H.R. 1654, H.R. 1762, H.R. 1869, H.R. 3059, S. 280, S. 554, and S. 625. No congressional action occurred on these bills.

In: Biennial Budgeting
Editor: Carolyn Douglas
ISBN: 978-1-63482-673-0

Chapter 2

BIENNIAL BUDGETING*

Roy T. Meyers

ABSTRACT

Should the Congress prepare a budget every two years rather than every year, as it does now? This proposed reform, known as biennial budgeting, has received increased attention in recent years. The Congressional Budget Office (CBO) prepared this paper in response to numerous inquiries about the subject.

The paper is divided into four Sections. The first provides background information on the annual character of the current process and a history of proposals to convert to multiyear budgeting. The second Section describes three bills that reflect different approaches to biennial budgeting.

The experiences of the states and of other countries with biennial budgeting are related in the third Section. The concluding Section analyzes the potential effects of converting from annual to biennial budgeting.

* This is an edited, reformatted and augmented version of a report issued by the Congressional Budget Office, February 1988.

SUMMARY

Biennial budgeting is the practice of preparing and adopting budgets for two-year periods. Nine bills to convert to biennial budgeting have been introduced in the 100th Congress.

The central rationale for biennial budgeting is that it would improve the efficiency of the Congressional budget process. Frustration with the current process is high: it is time-consuming, target dates are often missed, and repetitive decisions are made. The solution to these problems, according to proponents of biennial budgeting, is to prepare one budget instead of two over a two-year period. Having fewer budgets could reduce the delay and repetition that plague the current budget process, and could free time for other activities.

Two biennial budgeting approaches have been proposed-the "stretch" and "split-sessions" models. The stretch model would have the Congress prepare a budget for the biennium (the two-year fiscal period) over the two years of a Congress. The split-sessions model would have the Congress prepare a biennial budget during one year and conduct nonbudgetary activities in the other. The bills that take this approach begin the biennium on October 1 of either the odd year (the first year of a Congress) or the even year (the second year of a Congress). The stretch model would begin the biennium on October 1 of the even year.

Few statements can be made with much certainty about the effects of a conversion to biennial budgeting, except that this would be a radical change from the current process. Despite the permanence of much government spending, the *process* of formulating, enacting, and executing budgets is characteristically annual.

One way that biennial budgeting would depart significantly from current practices would be its restriction of certain activities to specified periods. Under the split-sessions model. the Congress is expected to forgo revising the budget during the nonbudgetary year. The pressure to revise the budget would often be strong, however, and no rules of the Congress exist that would prevent it from doing so. With split sessions, moreover, the specialized roles of the budget, appropriations, and oversight committees might leave these committees with significant periods of inactivity.

The stretch model assumes that having a longer period for making budgetary decisions will make missing target dates less likely. The accuracy of this assumption is questionable. Delay is probably inherent to budgeting because of the important decisions that are made in this comprehensive process. In addition, differences over budgetary goals between the Congress and the President, and between the House and the Senate, have been important causes of missed target dates. Biennial budgeting is likely to make it even more difficult to reach compromises over major policy differences, because the stakes will be higher with a two-year budget than with a one-year budget.

Expanding the horizon of the budget by a year will undoubtedly increase errors in budget projections, but the extent of this increase is uncertain. Deficit projection errors caused by economic forecast errors would likely be slightly larger for a biennial than for an annual budget. Deficit projection errors from inaccuracies in technical assumptions, while impossible to predict reliably, could be smaller for a biennial than for an annual budget.

Given that the Congress copes with a substantial amount of uncertainty now, the increase attributable to biennial budgeting might be bearable. In addition, the Congress could compensate for increased uncertainty by changing some of its current goals and procedures. It could accept the unpredictability of the economy, refraining from attempts to "fine-tune" spending and taxing in order to hit specific deficit or economic growth targets. When funding individual programs, it could adopt procedures that would reduce the demand for supplemental appropriations and rescissions.

The experiences of other governments suggest, however, that added uncertainty may at times be quite costly. Most states are subject to effective limits on spending and borrowing, and complying with these limits has become more difficult with the growing uncertainty of revenue streams This problem is one reason why the states have moved away *from* biennial budgeting-44 states used biennial budgeting in 1940, but only 19 do now. Many of the remaining biennial states have made major budget revisions in the off-years because of impending deficits. Biennial budgeting is infrequently used in other countries. No developed democracies currently practice biennial budgeting, and developing countries are encouraged to budget annually by multinational creditors.

Finally, biennial budgeting could limit cooperation between the executive and legislative branches by reducing their frequency of interaction. Cooperation might not decrease significantly were the Congress to use fully the time allocated for oversight activities. This would be consistent with the increasing use of oversight in recent years. Using oversight in place of appropriations might also improve the ability of the Congress to understand problems and monitor the Executive Branch.

This course would reduce the amount of influence that the Congress could exercise annually, however. The "must-pass" character of appropriations requires the Executive Branch to negotiate in good faith and to conform to previously enacted law. Therefore, forgoing annual appropriations would mean that the Congress would periodically do without its most coercive tool. In the absence of annual appropriation controls, the Congress might respond by writing legislation more restrictively for agencies that it did not trust. By eliminating agencies' flexibility, these "micromanagement" provisions could force them to act inefficiently. Yet, since it would often be difficult for the Congress to anticipate future conditions, agencies would probably be left with greater discretion than they currently enjoy.

In sum, this analysis suggests that biennial budgeting might not live up to expectations unless the Congress substantially changes its goals and behavior. It would have to accept increased uncertainty about budget outcomes, a reduced ability to be responsive to immediate concerns, and less influence from use of the appropriation process. If these changes were accepted, the Congress could reduce the number of repetitive votes on budget issues, and spend more time on policy planning and oversight. Biennial budgeting could also allow agencies and grantees to spend money more efficiently. But it would not eliminate the delays that come from negotiating important budget decisions.

If the Congress does not wish to change as radically as biennial budgeting would require, it could implement biennial budgeting selectively—for technically predictable and politically stable programs, for example. Although some flexibility might be lost by these actions, the Congress could compensate by subjecting currently mandatory programs to more frequent reviews.

SECTION I. BACKGROUND

In this paper, budgeting is defined as the consideration of budget resolutions, appropriation bills, and the portions of authorization bills that authorize or limit spending. Annual budgeting has been the general practice in the federal government. Interest in biennial budgeting has increased, however, and a number of multiyear budgeting reforms have been considered or adopted in recent years.

Annual Appropriations and Authorizations

Appropriations have been made annually since the 1st Congress, and with the adoption of the Budget and Accounting Act in 1921, the President was required to present appropriation requests at the beginning of each calendar year. The Congress routinely considers at least 14 appropriation bills (13 regular and 1 supplemental) each year.

The schedule for considering appropriation bills should not be confused with the time periods for which appropriations are made available. In the early years of the republic, most appropriations were available to an agency for only one year. The Congress now makes most appropriations available for periods longer than a year. In fiscal year 1985, 53 percent of appropriations were permanent in law. The remaining 47 percent were made through the annual appropriation process. Of these annual appropriations (excluding discretionary appropriations for the legislative and judicial branches and the Executive Office of the President), only about one-half (or one-quarter of all appropriations) were made available for only the upcoming budget year. The remaining were multiyear, no-year, or advance appropriations.[1] Thus, while budgeting decisions are made annually, the availability of budgeted funds covers various time periods.

Annual authorization of appropriations is currently a regular practice, but this was not the case three decades ago. Before 1959, only military construction, foreign aid, and the Atomic Energy Commission were authorized annually. With the passage of annual authorizations for the National Aeronautics and Space Administration and military procurement in 1959, the Congress began to rely on annual authorizations to increase its control of the Executive Branch. Annual authorizations also served the authorizing committees by enabling them to participate in budgetary decisions as frequently as the appropriations committees. By the 1970s, authorizations for the majority of discretionary appropriations were being considered annually, including authorizations for all defense and intelligence agencies, the Peace Corps, the Coast Guard, the National Science Foundation, the Department of Energy, the Department of Justice, and research and development for the Environmental Protection Agency. Not all of the annual authorizations have been enacted in each year, however. In 1987, for example, only a fifth of the nondefense discretionary appropriations that are frequently authorized annually were in fact authorized.[2] And like multiyear appropriations in annual appropriation bills, some authorizations enacted in annual authorization bills lasted for more than one year. Authorizations for specific military construction projects, for example, were routinely for two years.

The Congressional Budget Act of 1974

The schedule for considering authorizations and appropriations was of major interest during deliberations over the Congressional Budget Act. Two problems were thought to be most serious—the Congress routinely failed to pass appropriations before the beginning of the fiscal year, and the Congress often failed to pass authorizations until the beginning of the fiscal year was near, allowing little time for the appropriation process. The Congressional Budget Act included several provisions that were intended to reduce these delays. First, authorizations were scheduled for early consideration. Section 607 asked that the President submit requests for reauthorization by May 15 of the year *preceding* the year in which the authorization would begin.[3] This section also asked the President to submit multiyear authorization requests for new programs. Section 402 established a point of order against considering authorizations that had not been reported by May 15. This provision was intended to speed up consideration of authorizations. The same May 15 date was used as a target for completion of the first budget resolution, and Section 303 established a point of order against considering any bill providing new budget authority before the first budget resolution was adopted. Action on appropriations was intended to be completed by seven days after Labor Day, before the beginning of the fiscal year, which was changed to October 1.

Other multiyear provisions in the Budget Act required the Office of Management and Budget (OMB) and the Congressional Budget Office (CBO) to make five-year budget projections, and CBO to provide five-year cost estimates and scorekeeping reports for authorizing legislation and bills providing new budget authority, respectively. In subsequent years, the budget resolutions themselves were expanded to include multiyear projections. The first resolution for fiscal year 1980 included two years of out-year projections for the budgetary aggregates, though separate projections were made for the Senate and the House. By the first resolution for fiscal year 1982, the same projections were made for spending by budget function in both the House and the Senate.

The broader approach of biennial budgeting received little attention during the formulation of the act. Senator Bellmon proposed that each Congress be divided into a budgetary session and a legislative (nonbudgetary) session. Senator Nunn and Congressman Conyers separately proposed that appropriations and authorizations be considered on a staggered basis, with one-half of each being enacted each year. Only one proposal was put into the form of draft legislation. Senators Mondale and Javits proposed biennial budgeting in an amendment (# 601) to S. 1541, the bill being considered by the Senate Government Operations Committee, but the amendment was not accepted by the committee.

Increased Interest in Biennial Budgeting

The first biennial budgeting bill was introduced by Congressman Panetta in 1977.[4] This bill was reintroduced in 1979, and Senator Bumpers introduced another biennial budgeting bill in the same year. The bills were reintroduced in 1981, and other biennial bills were introduced in 1981 and 1982 by Senators Ford, Quayle, Roth, and Cochran. Hearings were held in these years by the Senate Governmental Affairs Committee and the House and Senate Budget Committees.[5]

Biennial budgeting was also considered from 1982 to 1984 by the Task Force on the Budget Process, chaired by Congressman Beilenson of the House Rules Committee. The task force considered four alternative proposals for reform of the budget process:

- The *single binding resolution* approach, which would have codified the procedural changes made to the budget process during its first decade, such as reconciliation after the first budget resolution.
- The *target resolution* approach, which was similar to the original process established by the Congressional Budget Act.
- The *omnibus budget bill* approach, which proposed that all appropriation bills, revenue bills, and reconciliation of direct spending be considered in one bill.
- The *biennial budgeting* approach.

The task force recommended the single binding resolution approach. It commented as follows on biennial budgeting:

> Biennial budgeting. The task force considered the possibility of stretching over a two-year period the entire process – budget resolution, appropriations bills, and authorizations – in order to lighten the Congress' annual workload and provide additional time for other important activities, such as oversight. There were two leading arguments against a two-year system: one was that it did not seem feasible to adopt a budget resolution for a two-year period, given the rapidness with which political and economic circumstance change. The other was concern about having one Congress

> make decisions that could be binding through a subsequent Congress. Furthermore, several variations of biennial budgeting have been proposed, and there is no consensus on which version would be the most practicable.
>
> The task force does endorse providing authorizations for periods of two or more years, as noted above. The task force also encourages the Government *(sic:* should be "General") Accounting Office and the Office of Management and Budget to study the feasibility of placing some annually financed programs on two-year funding. Such studies would give Congress a better basis for determining whether it should move to a biennial budget system in the future.[6]

The task force also recommended that committees report more multiyear and advance authorizations, and strongly favored dropping the May 15 reporting deadline for authorizations, believing it had proved ineffective. Furthermore, it wanted to allow consideration of appropriations after May 15 even if the budget resolution had not been adopted.

These and other recommendations made by the task force were accepted by the Rules Committee, and many of them were included in the Balanced Budget and Emergency Deficit Control Act of 1985 (popularly known as Gramm-Rudman-Hollings).

In particular, the timetable for considering the budget was accelerated. The President's budget submission was moved up to January 3, and the views and estimates reports from committees to February 25. The budget resolution was to be enacted by April 15, reconciliation by June 15, and appropriations by June 30 in the House.[7]

In the Senate, the 1984 Temporary Select Committee to Study the Senate Committee System, chaired by Senator Quayle (a cosponsor of Senator Ford's bill), recommended that a select committee be established to study the feasibility of biennial budgeting.

In 1985, Senator Quayle proposed an amendment to the fiscal year 1986 legislative branch appropriation bill to establish such a committee, but withdrew the amendment after Senator Domenici offered to hold joint Budget Committee and Governmental Affairs hearings on budget process reform.[8] With the passage of the Balanced Budget Act, however, attention shifted away from biennial budgeting and the hearings were never held.

The Experiment of Budgeting Biennially for Defense

The most significant move toward biennial budgeting has been the adoption in 1985 of the Nunn-McCurdy amendment to the fiscal year 1986 defense authorization bill (Public Law 99-145). This amendment is reprinted below.

> SEC. 1405. TWO-YEAR BUDGET CYCLE FOR THE DEPARTMENT OF DEFENSE
>
> (a) FINDINGS. The Congress finds that the programs and activities of the Department of Defense could be more effectively and efficiently planned and managed if funds for the Department were provided on a two-year cycle rather than annually.
>
> (b) REQUIREMENT FOR TWO-YEAR BUDGET PROPOSAL. The President shall include in the budget submitted to the Congress pursuant to section 1105 of title 31, United States Code, for fiscal year 1988 a single proposed budget for the Department of Defense and related agencies for fiscal years 1988 and 1989. Thereafter, the President shall submit a proposed two-year budget for the Department of Defense and related agencies every other year.
>
> (c) REPORT. Not later than April 1, 1986, the Secretary of Defense shall submit to the Committees on Armed Services and on Appropriations of the Senate and House of Representatives a report containing the Secretary's views on the following:
>
> (1) The advantages and disadvantages of operating the Department of Defense and related agencies on a two-year budget cycle.
>
> (2) The Secretary's plans for converting to a two-year budget cycle.
>
> (3) A description of any impediments (statutory or otherwise) to converting the operations of the Department of Defense and related agencies to a two-year budget cycle beginning with fiscal year 1988.

The Nunn-McCurdy amendment for a biennial budget was at first wholeheartedly embraced by the Department of Defense. Biennial budgeting for defense received additional endorsements from the President's Blue Ribbon Commission on Defense Management (the Packard Commission), the Center for Strategic and International Studies, and the Heritage Foundation. The President's fiscal year 1988 budget included separate appropriation requests for fiscal years 1988 and 1989 for accounts in the national defense function.

Biennial budgeting for defense quickly declined, however, as several of its initial proponents backed away from rapid implementation. In its April 1,

1986, report to the Congress that was mandated by Public Law 99-145, the Department of Defense stated:

> It is important to note that, although many have expressed support for the general concept of biennial budgeting, the concept has not been adequately defined. If not done carefully, it is conceivable that the transition of this idea to implementation may yield a process that would be unsatisfactory to everyone. This is particularly true in view of the current Gramm-Rudman-Hollings legislation that injects an element of uncertainty in the budget process, be it for one or two years' duration. The benefits that may be envisioned through biennial budgeting are perhaps obviated by the threat of Gramm-Rudman-Hollings imposed reductions.

In the Congress, Senator *Nunn* wrote the Senate Budget Committee on February 24,1987, to explain that:

> The (Armed Services] Committee is recommending a National Defense spending level only for fiscal year 1988 because the President's FY1988 Budget fails to meet the Gramm-Rudman deficit targets after FY1988. The Defense Department submitted a credible two-year budget for FY1988 and FY1989 as part of its FY1988-92 Five Year Defense Plan. Our Committee strongly supports the concept of shifting to a two-year budget. Unfortunately, the President has not told Congress how he plans to pay for his proposed level of Defense spending after FY1988 within the Gramm-Rudman deficit targets, making our job of recommending and adopting a two-year Defense budget extremely difficult.

The Senate passed a bill that authorized about 70 percent of the defense budget for two years. The House passed an annual authorization bill, however, leading the conference of the two committees to agree on an authorization bill that contained some authorizations for fiscal year 1989, but which authorized most programs for only fiscal year 1988. An annual appropriation bill for the Department was included in the continuing resolution.

Through most of 1987, the Department of Defense did not follow its regular schedule for preparing the budget request; instead, it planned to make an "implementation review" of the two-year request in order to prepare budget amendment, supplemental, and rescission requests for fiscal year 1989. However, shortly after the summit agreement was reached for spending plans for 1988 and 1989, Secretary of Defense Carlucci ordered the department to reduce its budget request for fiscal year 1989 by $33 billion.

The Current Situation

Dissatisfaction with the current process of budgeting has continued, and biennial budgeting is still being discussed as a possible solution.[9] Many Members of Congress have been pressed by the heavy work load that results from the overlapping actions taken during the annual appropriation and authorization processes. They have been embarrassed that the Congress has missed many budget process deadlines, and disappointed with the reliance in 1986 on an omnibus continuing resolution to provide appropriations for fiscal year 1987.[10] An additional impetus for the revival of interest in biennial budgeting was the Balanced Budget Act's ceiling on the budget year deficit, which gave an incentive to shift outlays from the budget year to the current or future years. Some Members believe that biennial budgeting, with its extension of the budget period to two years, would reduce or limit opportunities for such artificial savings.

The Administration took a small step toward biennial budgeting in the fiscal year 1988 budget by including planning estimates for fiscal *year* 1989 *for* nondefense accounts. In testimony before the House Government Operations Committee, OMB Director Miller stated that he would like to expand biennial budget requests to the whole budget. President Reagan has supported biennial budgeting in addresses on budget reform, but the Administration has not proposed or endorsed relevant legislation.

The Senate discussed biennial budgeting during consideration of the fiscal year 1988 budget resolution. Senator Roth proposed a sense of the Congress resolution that "the Congress should enact this year a biennial budget and appropriations process." The resolution was tabled by a vote of 53 to 45.[11] This was followed by inclusion of a biennial budgeting provision in the Balanced Budget Reaffirmation Act (Public Law 100-119). Section 201 stated:

> It is the sense of the Congress that the Congress should undertake an experiment with multiyear authorizations and 2-year appropriations for selected agencies and accounts. An evaluation of the efficacy and desirability of such experiment should be conducted at the end of the 2-year period. The appropriate committees are directed to develop a plan in consultation with the leadership of the House and Senate to implement this experiment.[12]

Senator Roth has introduced a bill reflecting this approach, which would convert the limitation on the administrative expenses of the Social Security Administration to a two-year limitation.[13]

The summit negotiations between the Congress and the President considered and rejected the adoption of biennial budgeting. However, the agreement reached in November set separate targets for spending for domestic, international, and defense categories for fiscal years 1988 and 1989. The agreement also specified that the President's budget and the budget resolution for fiscal year 1989 should be consistent with these targets, and pledged that supplementals will not be initiated "except in the case of dire emergency." Section 8001 of the Budget Reconciliation Act of 1987 (Public Law 100-203) established budget authority and outlay targets for defense and nondefense discretionary spending, and created enforcement procedures for these targets. Section 10621(b)(3) of the act stated that it was the sense of the Congress that it should undertake "an experimental multiyear authorization and 2-year appropriation for the Internal Revenue Service." This provision was intended for the process of funding the IRS for fiscal years 1989 and 1990.

SECTION II. MAJOR BIENNIAL BUDGET PROPOSALS OF THE 100TH CONGRESS

Three approaches to biennial budgeting have been proposed in the current Congress. Major bills that represent these approaches are: S. 416, cosponsored by Senators Roth and Domenici; S. 286, sponsored by Senator Ford; and H.R. 22, cosponsored by Congressmen Panetta and Regula.[1] This Section compares the bills' major features. Table 1 compares the target dates established by the three bills.

Three other bills contain, among other provisions, language identical to that in H.R. 22: H.R. 33, sponsored by Congressman Daub; H.R. 777, sponsored by Representative Lloyd; and H.R. 805, sponsored by Congressman Penny. Another bill, H.R. 1558, cosponsored by Congressmen Hutto and Lott, is similar in intent to H.R. 22. S. 1362, cosponsored by Senators Kassebaum and Inouye, includes a biennial budget proposal that is similar to S. 416. Finally, S. 832, sponsored by Senator Domenici, is an omnibus budget reform bill that incorporates the text of S. 416.

S. 416

S. 416 bears the closest resemblance to the existing budget process. Budgeting would take place in the first nine months of the first session (odd year) of a Congress, and the biennium would begin on October 1. The bill would delay submission of the President's budget to January 15 and return to the original Congressional Budget Act's dates for the views and estimates reports (March 15) and for reporting and passing the budget resolution (April 15 and May 15, respectively). Appropriation action would be completed in the House by the end of June, and all appropriation bills and the reconciliation bill would be enacted by September 30. The second session of the Congress would be devoted primarily to considering authorizations for the next biennium, though the President would be required to submit a revised budget for the biennium on January 15 of the even year (three and a half months after the beginning of the biennium). If S. 416 were passed, it would take effect on January 1, 1988. During 1988, the Congress would pass year-ahead authorizations and an annual budget for fiscal year 1989. The first biennial budget would be enacted in 1989.[2]

Table 1. Target Dates In Biennial Budgeting Bills

Date	S.416	S.286	H.R. 22
11/10		Current services	
	Congress Begins First Session-Odd Year		
1/3			Current services
1/15	President's biennial budget;	President's biennial budget;	President's biennial budget oversight begins
2/15	CBO report		
3/15	Views and estimates		
4/15	Budget resolution reported	CBO report	
5/15	Budget resolution completed;	Views and estimates	
6/1	Appropriation bills reported in House		
6/15	Appropriation bills completed in House	Budget resolution reported	

Table 1. (Continued)

Date	S.416	S.286	H.R. 22
6/30	Appropriation bills reported in Senate		Committees complete oversight reports
7/1		Committees report authorizations of new budget authority	Committees begin legislative work
9/30	Appropriations and reconciliation finished		
10/1	Biennium begins		
10/31			Views and estimates
11/10			CBO report
11/30			Budget resolution reported
12/1		Congress finishes authorizations of new budget authority	
12/31			Committees report authorizations of new budget authority
	Congress Begins Second Session-Even Year		
1/3		Current services	
1/15	President's revised budget for biennium	President's revised budget for biennium	President's revised budget for biennium
3/1			Congress finishes authorizations of new budget authority
3/31	CBO report	Spending bills reported in House; CBO report	Budget resolution completed
4/15		Spending bills reported in Senate	Appropriation bills reported
6/15		Second budget resolution reported	

Date	S.416	S.286	H.R. 22
7/15		Congress completes spending bills	
8/1		Second budget resolution completed	
Labor Day plus 7 days		Congress completes spending bills	
9/25		Congress completes reconciliation	Congress completes reconciliation
10/1		Biennium begins	Biennium begins
Adjournment	Authorizations of new budget authority for next biennium fini shed		

Source: Congressional Budget Office.

S. 286

The process set out by S. 286 resembles the original Congressional Budget Act process stretched out over a two-year period. The President would begin the process by submitting a budget on January 15 of the first session (odd year) of a Congress for the biennium beginning on October 1 of the second session (even year). The first year would be devoted to passage of a budget resolution (by the end of July) and the authorization of new budget authority (by December 1). The President would submit a revised budget on January 15. Bills that provided budget and entitlement authority would have to be reported by March 31 in the House and April 15 in the Senate. A second budget resolution would be completed by August 1, and a reconciliation bill might then be necessary and would be scheduled for passage by September 25. One hundred hours of debate would be allowed on a reconciliation bill in the Senate. If S. 286 were passed, it would become effective at the start of the 101st Congress. The bill establishes a transition to a biennial process by having the Congress enact an annual budget for fiscal year 1990 and a biennial budget for fiscal years 1991 and 1992.[3]

H.R. 22

H.R. 22 proposes the greatest departure from the previous or the existing budget process. Like S.286, it requires the President to submit a budget on January 15 of the first session of a Congress for the biennium beginning on October 1 of the second session. The Congress would not take any action on the budget for most of the first year, however. The first six months would be reserved for oversight activities. On July 1, committees would begin considering authorizing legislation, and would have to report authorizations of new budget authority by the end of the *year*. These bills would have to be enacted by the following March 10.

Preparation of the budget resolution would begin with the submission of views and estimates reports by October 31. After receiving a Congressional Budget Office report on November 10, the Budget Committees would report budget resolutions by November 30, and then wait for a revised President's budget on January 15. The budget resolution would be completed by March 31. The rest of the period until September 25 would be devoted to passing spending bills and reconciliation. If H.R. 22 were passed, it would become effective with the 101st Congress. The bill as drafted neglects to allow for a transition year in 1989 for the fiscal year 1990 budget.

Biennial Budgeting Timetables

Though this paper is not a detailed review of the specifics of the biennial bills, this section discusses a few issues regarding the feasibility of the bills' timetables.

H.R. 22

This bill would ask that the President's budget be submitted on January 15, but committee views and estimates reports would not be due until October 31. The CBO report would be released on November 10 and the budget resolution reported by November 30. The President would then release his revised budget for the upcoming biennium on January 15.

This schedule would seem to encourage reestimates during preparation of the budget resolution. The views and estimates reports would be based on a President's budget submitted nine months earlier and would not benefit from the CBO report, which would be released 10 days later. The budget resolution would be reported but not passed before the President's revised budget was submitted. The revisions in the budget would probably require the Budget Committees to revise their reported resolutions. In contrast to this long period *for* preparing the budget resolution, H.R. 22 allows only 15 days from the adoption of the budget resolution to the date that appropriation bills are supposed to be reported.

S. 286

This bill establishes long periods between each target date. The CBO, for example, is given three months to produce its report after the President's budget is submitted. The major timing issue presented by this bill relates to enforcement. The bill repeals many of the enforcement procedures that were formally adopted by the Congress in the Balanced Budget Act. It returns to the original process in which the first budget resolution would not be binding and the second resolution would be completed after spending bills were passed. Reconciliation would follow the second resolution in the two months (August and September) before the beginning of the biennium. The Congress had difficulty under this procedure enforcing the deficit reductions planned in the first resolution. That the Congress could do any better using the same procedure, but over a two-year period, is not self-evident.

S. 416

Like H.R. 22, this bill allows a short period from passage of the budget resolution to reporting of appropriation bills. It is even more optimistic in expecting that appropriation bills could be completed after 15 days in the House.

None of the bills include in their model timetables a period for consideration of supplemental appropriation bills or rescission requests. Both H.R. 22 and S. 286 allow a simple waiver of the deadline for reporting appropriation bills.

SECTION III. STATE AND INTERNATIONAL EXPERIENCES WITH BIENNIAL BUDGETING

Arguments for and against federal biennial budgeting often proceed by analogy with budgeting in the states. This is particularly true in the Congress because many Members and Senators have had experience as state legislators or governors and would like to try at the federal level the procedures that they became familiar with at home. International experiences with biennial budgeting are less frequently invoked, primarily because it is rarely used in democratic countries. Multiyear planning, on the other hand, has gained momentum gradually.

The States

A recent survey by the National Conference of State Legislatures (NCSL) concluded that 31 states will adopt annual budgets in 1987, and 19 states will adopt or be operating under biennial budgets (see Table 2).[1] NCSL's definition of biennial budgeting requires that appropriations be provided for two years, either as separate appropriations for each of the two years (as is done by 14 states) or as a single appropriation (five states). A state is not classified as biennial if the governor proposes a biennial budget but the legislature appropriates for only one year. Florida has followed this practice in recent years. Other aspects of NCSL's basic categorization may result in an overestimate of the prevalence of biennial budgeting. In 11 of the biennial states – all but one of the biennial states with annual sessions – the NCSL found that major annual reviews of the biennial budget are anticipated by provisions of the states' constitutions or are traditionally performed. In Ohio, for example, a committee of the legislature has made extensive modifications to the enacted budget during the off-year. In some of the states whose constitutions do not anticipate revisions or where annual reviews have not traditionally been made, fiscal crises have led to amendments of biennial budgets. Texas is one example.

Table 2. Frequency of Budgeting in States

State	Frequency	Changes in Frequency[a]	Revisions Possible	Availability of Appropriations
Alabama	Annual	A'76		
Alaska	Annual			
Arizona	Annual			
Arkansas	Biennial		No	One Year
California	Annual			
Colorado	Annual			
Connecticut	Annual	A"71		
Delaware	Annual			
Florida	Annual			

State	Frequency	Changes in Frequency[a]	Revisions Possible	Availability of Appropriations
Georgia	Annual	A'74		
Hawaii	Biennial	B'71	Yes	One Year
Idaho	Annual			
Illinois	Annual			
Indiana	Biennial	A'75; B'78	Yes	One Year
Iowa	Annual	A'75;B'79;A'83		
Kansas	Annual			
Kentucky	Biennial		No	One Year
Louisiana	Annual			
Maine	Biennial		Yes	One Year
Maryland	Annual			
Massachusetts	Annual			
Michigan	Annual			
Minnesota	Biennial	A'73;B'75	Yes	One Year
Mississippi	Annual			
Missouri	Annual	A"72		
Montana	Biennial		No	One Year
Nebraska	Biennial	A"72;B'87	Yes	One Year
Nevada	Biennial		No	One Year
New Hampshire	Biennial		No	One Year
New Jersey	Annual			
New Mexico	Annual			
New York	Annual			
North Carolina	Biennial	A'73; B"75	Yes	Two Year
North Dakota	Biennial		No	Two Year
Ohio	Biennial		Yes	One Year
Oklahoma	Annual			
Oregon	Biennial		No	Two Year
Pennsylvania	Annual			
Rhode Island	Annual			
South Carolina	Annual			
South Dakota	Annual	-		
Tennessee	Annual	A'70		
Texas	Biennial		No	One Year
Utah	Annual			
Vermont	Annual	A"78		
Virginia	Biennial		Yes	One Year
Washington	Biennial		Yes	Two Year

Table 2. (Continued)

State	Frequency	Changes in Frequency[a]	Revisions Possible	Availability of Appropriations
West Virginia	Annual			
Wisconsin	Biennial		Yes	One Year
Wyoming	Biennial		Yes	Two Year

Source: Barbara Yondorf, "Annual Versus Biennial Budgeting: The Arguments, the Evidence" (National Conference of State Legislatures, January 36,1987).

[a]."A" signifies a change from biennial to annual; '13" signifies a change from annual to bienniaL

The states have moved away from biennial budgeting in the past 40 years; 44 states followed the practice in 1940. The "Changes in Frequency" column in Table 2 shows the states that have shifted to annual or biennial budgeting since 1970. One reason for the movement away from biennial budgeting was the professionalization of state legislatures, which accelerated in the 1960s and 1970s. With larger and more competent staffs and with annual rather than biennial sessions, some legislatures felt capable of reviewing budgets annually (Missouri and Connecticut are examples). The growth in federal grant revenues gave state legislatures an incentive to participate annually in the allocation of these funds. Legislatures have also temporarily used annual budgets when the governor was not a member of the majority party in the legislature, and returned to biennial budgets when partisan control became unified (Iowa and North Carolina are examples).

Another cause of the shift to annual budgets has been the increased sensitivity of state budgets to economic cycles (largely because of increased reliance on the income tax as a major revenue source), coupled with balanced budget limits. Under biennial budgeting, large unpredicted shortfalls in revenues as well as smaller unpredicted increases in outlays *for* uncontrollable benefit programs have often created deficits in state budgets. When states had insufficient cash reserves to finance tkiese deficits, they had to revise their budgets during the biennium to meet their balanced budget limits. Repeated situations like this led some states to convert formally to annual budgeting, the form of budgeting they were practicing in a de facto manner (Vermont, Alabama, and Florida are examples).

The states that have converted to biennial budgeting have done so for a number of reasons. Hawaii wanted to reserve the nonbudget year for program reviews, and Nebraska returned to biennial budgeting to increase control of out-year spending. The Minnesota legislature passed an annual budget in 1974, but a citizen referendum required a return to biennial budgeting.

Other Countries

The experiences of other countries contrast markedly with those of the states.[2] Budgeting has been an annual process in almost all of the countries of the noncommunist world. Among Western European democracies, only Spain has a history of biennial budgeting. The practice was dropped there in the early 1970s before the end of the Franco regime. Some developing countries with Spanish heritages, such as Peru, have also budgeted biennially in the past, and Bahrain currently has a biennial budget.

The prevalence of annual budgeting in other democratic countries is partially explained by their constitutional structures. Many democratic countries have parliamentary structures in which the political executive is drawn from the legislature. This executive is given the primary responsibility for developing the government's budget as well as managing it. The budget is used as a method of setting forth the government's program and as a test of the government's support. It is usually ratified by the parliament with few changes. When the governing majority in parliament is unstable, however, the budget vote may also provoke a parliamentary crisis by which the government may fall. In these countries, the annual opportunity to test the support for the government is widely thought to be a condition for democratic government.

This purpose of the budget is not important in nondemocratic countries. These countries tend to have more centrally planned economies and would be more likely to use biennial budgeting. Yet nondemocratic countries also tend to be underdeveloped and undiversified; their economies are subject to great variations in economic conditions. The resulting swings in the finances of the governments of developing countries have been frequent, necessitating annual revisions of long-term plans. The International Monetary Fund recommends that developing countries have annual budgeting processes in order to cope with these uncertainties.

Though few countries have attempted biennial budgeting, many have expanded the time horizon of budget planning estimates. This move to multiyear *planning* has been gradual, gaining momentum after the first oil price shock in 1973. Support for multiyear planning has been based largely on the realization that a sizable portion of budgets are transfer payments, and that these payments are long-term budget commitments that erode the annual flexibility of the budget. Multiyear planning estimates have been seen as a useful informational method of controlling these commitments.

Conclusion

If the United States were to adopt biennial budgeting, it would be the only democratic country to follow this practice. The international preference for annual budgeting does not necessarily indicate that biennial budgeting would not work for the U.S. government, however. Because of the unique constitutional structure and experimental political culture of the United States, the experiences of other countries are not directly relevant.

Comparisons to the experiences of states may be more relevant, as the states share the nation's political culture. Most comparisons between state and federal governments would lead one to make negative inferences about the prospects of biennial budgeting. Economic uncertainty and divided partisan control – factors that have caused many states to drop biennial budgeting – are also present at the federal level. In addition, the special characteristics of the federal government may make annual budgeting preferable. The Congress has a greater constitutional responsibility for developing budgets than most state legislatures, and the federal government has a larger and more complicated budget and a different economic role than the states. Only three of the ten largest states use biennial budgeting – North Carolina, Ohio, and Texas – and states that use biennial budgeting are on average smaller in population than those that use annual budgeting.[3]

Yet 19 states continue to budget biennially, which suggests that biennial budgeting can work if certain conditions are present. Unfortunately, studies of state experiences with biennial budgeting have not clearly identified these conditions. Such studies have typically consisted of surveys of state officials about the advantages and disadvantages of biennial and annual budgeting. Not surprisingly, officials tend to prefer current processes.

SECTION IV. POTENTIAL EFFECTS OF CONVERTING TO BIENNIAL BUDGETING

What is the optimal period for a budget process? In a search for the optimal period, it is easier to find losing candidates than to agree on the winner. A short period—a monthly budget process, for example – would create continuous uncertainty about government policies Monthly budget votes would be repetitive, and would leave no time to plan or to conduct oversight. In contrast, a longer period – a five-year budget process, for example—would reduce this work load. But unanticipated events and shifts in political priorities would occur frequently during the five years, making the budget obsolete and creating pressure for revisions.

Between the inflexibility of a five-year budget and the inefficient uncertainty of a monthly budget lie annual and biennial budgeting. Proponents of biennial budgeting say that annual budgeting is nearly as unworkable as the hypothetical process of monthly budgeting. They claim that the present process features repetitive votes on the same subject, both within the year and from one year to another. Repetitive votes cause delays in making budgetary decisions that must he made, such as appropriation bills, and also crowd out other activities, such as conducting oversight and considering authorization bills.

Given these problems, proponents offer biennial budgeting as a solution. They believe that recipients of grants will be able to spend funds more efficiently with the extra year of notice made available by a biennial budget. Management of agencies is also projected to benefit, as agencies would have to prepare and defend a budget only once every two years. Agencies might also be able to purchase some goods and services at lower costs, because they could buy in larger batches and offer longer-term contracts than annual budgeting permits.

Flexibility is the base of annual budgeting's support. Annual budgeting allows quick responses to changed economic conditions, to new policy goals, to shifts in public opinion, and to election results. The Congress has also found it to be useful for monitoring and influencing the Executive Branch.

If shifting to a biennial budget schedule would gain some certainty at the cost of some flexibility, how large is this trade-off likely to be? This Section provides some tentative answers to this question, and describes other trade-offs associated with a conversion to biennial budgeting. The analytical method is to posit four widely held goals for the budget process. These goals are:

- Allocating time efficiently to different activities, such as *planning,* budgeting, and conducting oversight;
- Completing preparation of the budget by the target date;
- Being appropriately responsive to changed conditions;
- Maintaining the proper influence of the Congress on policy.

The Section analyzes how lengthening the period of budget preparation might affect the attainment of these goals.

Allocate Time Efficiently to Different Activities

The Congress essentially undertakes three types of activities in the budget process – it gathers information about the problems the country is facing and authorizes programs to address these problems, it allocates funds to these programs, and it monitors the Executive Branch's implementation of its policy decisions. These activities often overlap; the Congress, for example, may learn about problems and the implementation of previous decisions as it considers appropriation requests.

How would the shift to a biennial schedule affect the performance of these activities? Proponents of biennial budgeting hope that some of the time now spent on budget formulation could be freed for oversight, authorizations, and district visits. This change in the mix of Members' activities could improve the quality of their work.

A distinction between biennial budgeting bills is helpful at this point. Both H.R. 22 and S. 416 would have the Congress schedule budgetary and nonbudgetary activities in different periods – an approach referred to here as the "split-sessions" approach. ("Nonbudgetary" in this context includes bills that authorize new budget authority.) S. 286 would have the Congress formulate a two-year budget over a two-year period, allowing nonbudgetary and budgetary activities to be interspersed during this time—referred to here as the "stretch" approach.

The split-sessions approach assumes that the Congress would postpone budgetary action on issues new to its agenda such as drug abuse or the plight of the homeless if these issues arose during a non-budgetary year. One supplemental appropriation bill would be expected in the nonbudgetary year, but it would be used only to provide appropriations for true emergencies. The split-sessions model similarly expects that the Congress would not conduct oversight during a budget year, though exceptions could be made for major scandals or controversies.

This approach might not succeed unless the Congress were to revise significantly its rules of procedure. The current rules would not provide a formal means of limiting consideration of spending bills during nonbudgetary periods, and in the absence of such rules, there would be frequent attempts to amend the budget during nonbudgetary periods. Such limiting rules could take various forms, including not allowing the Congress to consider budgetary matters during nonbudgetary periods unless the President requested such action, and limiting supplemental appropriations to project-specific deficiency appropriations or to cases in which statutorily defined "emergency" conditions have been met.[1]

Implementing limiting rules, such as defining "true" emergencies ahead of time, would be difficult. The split-sessions bills do not propose any such rules, and few of the states with biennial budgets and annual sessions have them. Some states that do not revise the budget during the off-year have relied instead on self-restraint, particularly when the nonbudgetary period immediately precedes an election. Others have been lucky, not being presented with unforeseen revenue losses that would have caused balanced budget requirements to be violated.

Split sessions imply substantial modifications to committee activities as well. The current committee structure gives specialized roles to various committees. The Budget Committees spend most of their time preparing and adopting the budget, and relatively little in monitoring spending by the agencies. The Appropriations Committees monitor spending, but almost always in the context of appropriating more funds. The House Government Operations and Senate Governmental Affairs Committees and the subcommittees of many other standing committees specialize in oversight. Unless these committees' responsibilities are changed, the Budget and Appropriations Committees are expected to be inactive during the nonbudgetary periods, as are the oversight committees during budgetary periods.

These potential changes in rules and committee activities heighten the importance of determining whether the process of making budgetary allocations has in fact crowded out authorizing legislation and oversight. The relationship between the budget process and the frequency of authorizing legislation is discussed in the last section. Regarding oversight, research by Joel Aberbach suggests that oversight has not been discouraged by the Congressional budget process. Aberbach compiled data for the number of total and oversight committee hearing days in the first six months of odd years from 1961 to 1983, excluding 1979.[2] Table 3 shows these data. The time-series shows a sharp increase in the proportion of days devoted to oversight from 1973 to 1975, and another sharp increase from 1981 to 1983. In 1983, a full quarter of hearing days were for oversight, more than double the proportion in 1973. Aberbach concludes that this growth in oversight activities is the result of a variety of factors: budget deficits, public discontent with government performance, Congressional concern about the usurpation of legislative powers by the Executive Branch, and the availability of more Congressional staff to carry out oversight.[3]

Aberbach counted as oversight hearings only those in which the "review of administrative actions" was the main activity. Reauthorization hearings were excluded. Many advocates of biennial budgeting, however, define oversight much more broadly. Under H.R. 22, for example, the "oversight period" during the first six months of a Congress would be devoted to reviewing policy goals and results. All the bills would have the Congress establish policy and program goals in advance authorizing legislation before the budget is considered.

A period set aside for taking stock and planning could be helpful for the Congress, which often focuses much of its energy on the issue of the moment. Similarly, advance authorizations might produce more informed appropriation decisions. These types of scheduling reforms view the Congress as an institution that could follow a very structured process for solving problems. But the role of the Congress as a sounding board for the public's interests may make a structured schedule unattainable.

Table 3. Bearing and Meeting Activities of Congressional Committees, January 1-July 4

Year	Total Days	Oversight Days	Oversight as Percent of Total
1961	1,789	146	8.2
1963	1,820	159	8.7
1965	2,055	141	6.9
1967	1,797	171	9.5
1969	1,804	217	12.0
1971	2,063	187	9.1
1973	2,513	290	11.5
1975	2,552	459	18.0
1977	3,053	537	17.6
1981	2,222	434	19.5
1983	2,331	587	25.2

Source: Joel D. Aberbach, *Keeping* a *Watchful Eye: The Politics of Congressional Oversight* (Washington, D.C.: Brookings Institution, forthcoming). Data for 1981 and 1983 are subject to final revision.

Note: Activities of Appropriations, Rules, Administration, and Joint Committees have been excluded. Data for 1979, 1985, and 1987 are currently being coded.

Complete Preparation of the Budget by the Target Date

The stretch model would spread budget formulation over a two-year period, giving more time for each stage to be completed. This approach assumes that target dates are missed because there is not enough time between each date—for example, when the budget resolution is late, this leads to unpassed appropriation bills and a continuing resolution. Preparing a budget over two years could allow more time for consultation, and make it more likely that decisions would be made on time.

Though the current schedule may be a cause of the time-consuming and repetitive nature of the budget process, other factors are probably even more important. One structural barrier to quick and binding decisions is the bicameral requirement that the House and Senate agree on all laws. Another is the separation of powers. Some missed target dates and repetitive votes clearly can be attributed to the difficulty of reaching a compromise between the strongly held positions of the President and the Congress. Biennial budgeting is not likely to facilitate such a compromise. Instead, it might increase the difficulty of reaching a compromise if agreements had to be negotiated for two years rather than for one. With the stakes higher, a two-year budget negotiation might take longer than two separate one-year negotiations. To repeat an observation made above, some states, have found annual budgeting more useful than their traditional biennial practices during periods of divided partisan control.

Other causes of repetition and delay may be more subject to change. The Congress is a legislature, to which each Member comes with one vote and a presumptive equal say in decisions. A natural result is that the Congress uses a decentralized form of internal organization, distributing decisionmaking powers widely among its Members. It does this in several ways. It divides its responsibilities among authorizing committees and appropriations committees, and these committees make similar types of decisions. The Congress also follows a very complicated budget process that is intended to control the decisions made in the authorization and appropriation processes. Delay and repetition might be reduced by adopting another form of internal organization and another budgeting procedure. In other words, in contrast to biennial budgeting, which would have the Congress prepare fewer budgets, the Congress might make fewer decisions during budget preparation.

The "fewer decisions" approach is embodied in a number of reform proposals, two of which will be described here generally. Both reforms would centralize power over budgetary decisions. In one approach, the Congress would combine the appropriations and authorizations committees and processes. In another, the Congress would adopt an omnibus budget procedure that would combine the aggregate budget resolution, appropriation bills, and reconciliation into a single bill.

Combined Authorizations and Appropriations Committees

A widespread belief is that the appropriations and authorizing committees should have separate and different roles. The authorizing committees are supposed to make substantive policy by establishing goals and designing programs, and the appropriations committees are supposed to make line-item reviews of agency budgets and then provide appropriations. House and Senate rules establish various points of order to encourage the separation of these activities.

In practice, there has been and is a great deal of blurring of the appropriation and authorization processes.[4] Both processes currently are used to set policy and allocate funds. Policy is set in appropriation bills through riders. Such "legislative" language in appropriation bills is technically subject to a point of order, but this obstacle is often overcome through waivers or by placing legislative language in continuing resolutions to which the point of order does not apply. Authorizing bills provide permanent appropriations and other *forms* of "backdoor" spending. In addition, authorizing bills often set line-item floors and ceilings on the amounts that may be appropriated.[5]

It is quite difficult to measure the extent to which the appropriation bills "make policy" and the authorization bills allocate funds. One method is to compare the forms of decisions made during the two processes. These forms are quite similar in the defense area. Annual authorizations and appropriations are routinely enacted for defense programs, and the committees make decisions using the same account and program structure. In contrast, the forms of nondefense authorization and appropriation decisions are often dissimilar. Most authorizations for nondefense discretionary appropriations are enacted for multiyear periods or are permanent, and the line-item units of authorizations often do not directly correspond to the lump-sum appropriation account structure. An initial conclusion, then, is that the overlap between appropriations and authorizations is probably greatest in the defense area.

Advocates of consolidation argue, however, that the similarity of the forms of outcomes or of the outcomes themselves is not that important. In theory, the Congress relies on committees to reap the advantages of specialization—expertise and an efficient division of labor. These advantages are not fully realized when two committees are established to deal with the same topic and when their bills are considered separately. When the two committees agree on policy goals, there would seem to be no benefit from first considering the authorization bill and then considering the appropriation bill. This duplication is simply a waste of time if similar amendments to each bill can be proposed from the floor. When the two committees disagree over policy, the case against duplication is still strong, if the bills can be freely amended on the floor. In this case, duplication encourages conflict, which slows up the process. Those who find the current degree of overlap to_ be large and unnecessary suggest that consolidation of the appropriations and authorizations committees and processes is an obvious way of increasing decisionmaking efficiency.[6]

The opposing view accepts "duplication," to the extent that it is admitted to exist, as beneficial. Redundancy of processes is useful, it is said, to reverse policy direction when conditions unexpectedly change, to reconsider a close division on a controversial issue, or to hold the Executive Branch to a bargain. Furthermore, supporters of the status quo claim that the different forms of appropriation and authorization decisions indicate that the two processes do not substantially overlap. They believe that the two types of committees bring different perspectives and skills to their tasks, and that the resulting competition among committees produces better outcomes. Finally, committee memberships, leadership positions, and staffs are valuable assets to Members, as are committee jobs to staffers. Any reform plan would have to promise substantial benefits to offset the costs of lost committee seniority and other assets.[7]

An Omnibus Budget Procedure

The other approach to making fewer decisions within the budget process is the omnibus budget procedure (also known as the Obey plan, after its main sponsor, Congressman Obey). In this procedure, the House Budget Committee would report a budget plan by April 15. This plan would serve as a guide for committee actions, but it would not be debated and voted on the floor. The committees would report separate bills for appropriations, revenues, and direct spending programs, and these bills would be packaged into an omnibus bill by the House Rules Committee. The bill would then be considered on the floor, and the House Budget Committee could offer privileged amendments to the titles of the omnibus bill that exceeded the targets in the budget plan.[8]

The essence of the omnibus reform is that there would be no vote on the House Budget Committee's plan. Because the current budget resolution is only a guideline for further action, the Congress sometimes considers the same issues twice—once during preparation of the budget resolution, and again when the actual budget is passed. (The debate may actually occur three times for programs being authorized in that year.) The votes on programmatic issues in the budget resolution are said to delay its adoption as well as slow consideration of appropriation bills. The omnibus reformers would have the Congress discard point of order and reconciliation enforcement procedures and vote only on actual budget allocations.

Opponents of the omnibus procedure suggest that it would not be workable. Spending committees would probably not feel bound to stay within the Budget Committee's plan unless the committees had endorsed it with a floor vote. Because the omnibus bill would be "must" legislation, it likely would attract many unrelated amendments. Some believe that it would be difficult to construct a majority for an omnibus bill because of objectionable provisions; others fear that logrolling would increase the totals of the omnibus bill.

Many Members and the President complain about the current reliance on the similar continuing resolution procedure. Besides the costs of brinksmanship, the difficulty of understanding and amending continuing resolutions disturbs those who are not members of the Appropriations Committees. From President Reagan's perspective, omnibus bills make it more difficult to exercise the veto and thus strengthen the need for an item veto.[9]

Regardless of whether these "fewer decision" reforms or a stretch model of biennial budgeting is adopted, delay and repetition in budgeting will not be eliminated. The famous "Parkinson's Law," which states that "Work expands to fill the time available for its completion," has a corollary: "A budget decision is not made until a deadline approaches." Delay and repetition are endemic to budgeting, because budgeting is a comprehensive process that resolves macro and micro goals into practical plans.

Even postponing the beginning of the fiscal year did not foster completing appropriation bills on time. Prior to the Congressional Budget Act, late enactment of appropriation bills was a continual problem – 46 percent of regular appropriation bills were enacted after the beginning of the fiscal year from 1968 to 1973.[10] The Congress – acting on the belief that when a deadline is routinely not met, permanently extending that deadline will solve the problem – moved the beginning of the fiscal year from July 1 to October 1.

Yet, appropriation bills are still not completed by the beginning of the fiscal year.

Additional evidence that repetition and delay cannot be avoided is seen in the budgeting experiences of the Executive Branch. Budget iterations between the Office of Management and Budget and agencies, which are similar to what is called duplication in the Congress, are frequent. A good example in this Administration has been the continual battle over defense spending, which started each year with the planning targets and continued all the way through the Director's Review.

The Executive Branch has also often found it difficult to meet the dates set out in its budget preparation schedule.

Be Appropriately Responsive to Chanced Conditions

The Congress is first and foremost a political body, designed to represent the interests and desires of the public. It consequently often revises previous decisions when public opinion changes. Given this special characteristic of the Congress, determining when to revise decisions becomes a balancing act. If the Congress were to make irreversible decisions, it would be foreclosing the opportunity for the public to change its mind (as the public itself changed its composition). Yet, if it were to always allow the national mood – which is often quite variable – to be quickly expressed as policy, it would be making "decisions" that would never stick.

The Congress responds not only to changes in public opinion, but also to macroeconomic, programmatic, and other political events. Only one type of event follows a completely predictable schedule: elections. The biennial budgeting bills differ in their choice of whether the biennium should begin before or after an election.

Both H.R. 22 and S. 286 schedule adoption of the budget just before an election. By placing these dates so closely together, these bills might clarify the policy choices that each party presents to the voters. On the other hand, if the electorate dislikes these choices and votes the majority party out of office, the new majority would theoretically be unable to adopt its program for two years. In the past, election results have had significant effects on budget priorities, particularly when a change in Presidential administrations occurs. It is likely, therefore, that the new majority would completely revise the recently adopted budget.

In contrast, S. 416 would have the Congress adopt a budget on a date that is roughly a year after an election and a year before an election. This schedule would allow the Congress to adopt a budget that reflected an election mandate, and permit the public to evaluate the Congress on the basis of a year's operation of this budget. But an upcoming election, particularly one coincident with a recession, might lead the Congress to revise the budget during the nonbudget year.[11]

The timing and magnitude of other events that might lead to Congressional action are harder to predict. By expanding the length of the budget period from one to two years, projection errors are likely to increase. Larger errors will increase pressure on the Congress to take action. If the Congress responds, some of the reductions in work load expected from biennial budgeting will not be realized.

The greatest source of uncertainty in budget estimates is the inherent unpredictability of the economy. To estimate the effect of making a two-year forecast on the accuracy of budget estimates, a simulation test used in the Congressional Budget Office's August 1987 report, *The Economic and Budget Outlook: An Update,* was extended for another year.[12] Table 4 shows the results. This test used a time-series model to forecast gross national product (GNP) for fiscal years 1988 and 1989. For 1988, simulating the time-series model 5,000 times (by introducing alternative random shocks) produced a standard deviation for GNP forecasts of $193 billion. The standard deviation is a statistical measure of the dispersion of individual forecasts around the average. It indicates that, given certain assumptions, GNP forecasts will differ from the actual GNP by less than $193 billion about 68 percent of the time. The same procedure produced a standard deviation of $226.6 billion for the fiscal year 1988-1989 biennium These uncertainty ranges may be translated into ranges for revenue estimates by using a rule of thumb that shows that a $100 billion error in estimating the GNP will tend to result in a $23 billion error in revenues.

This produces a standard deviation for revenue estimates of $44 billion for the first year and $52 billion for the biennium Because actual CBO forecast methodologies differ from the mechanical methods used in this test, the results should be understood as illustrative of the increased uncertainty in GNP forecasts under biennial budgeting, not as a prediction of CBO's likely performance.[13]

Table 4. Simulation of uncertainty in forecasts of gross national product and revenues for fiscal years 1988 and 1989 (all figures in billions of current dollars, except CV)

	Gross National Product		Revenues	
Fiscal Year	Mean	Standard Deviation	Standard Deviation	Coefficient of Variation (CV) [a]
1988	4,759.4	192.6	44.3	1.79
1989	5,093.3	275.3	63.3	3.42
Two-Year Average	4,926.4	226.6	62.1	2.40

Source: Congressional Budget Office calculations based on data in CBO, *The Economic and Budget Outlook: An Update* (August 1987), and on CEO simulations of a time-series model for forecasting GNP for fiscal years 1988 and 1989.

Note: The correlation between fiscal years 1988 and 1989 is 0.87.

[a]The coefficient of variation (CV) is the variance of revenues divided by the mean of revenues. The CV is a scale-free number.

A concrete example of the potential effect of economic uncertainty on biennial budget projections comes from CBO's most recent budget projection.[14] In November 1987, the fiscal year 1989 budget baseline deficit was estimated to be $186 billion. This estimate was based on CBO's August economic assumptions. The Congress then passed legislation that yielded $36 billion in savings for fiscal year 1989. In February, however, CBO projected the fiscal year 1989 baseline deficit to be $176 billion, an increase of $26 billion from the November baseline adjusted for enacted legislation. This increase was caused primarily by a forecast of slower growth in the economy. If a similar forecast is used by OMB on July 15, 1988, the Congress would need to make additional cuts beyond those envisioned in the summit agreement in order to prevent sequestration.[15]

The likely change in projection errors for individual programs is much harder to predict.[16] Some out-year budget projections for programs could become more realistic under biennial budgeting. Some agency budget estimates currently are too low, apparently because the agencies believe that it would be politically unwise to show the likely long-run costs of programs. In other cases, agency estimates are too high, sometimes to prompt agency contract officers to speed up operations. The incentives to make such misestimates would probably be reduced if appropriations were routinely made for two years. In addition, program characteristics would allow some projection errors to cancel out in two years that would not in one year. Spendout rates for procurement programs could exhibit this effect. For other programs, including many entitlement programs, errors would tend to cumulate.

Increased errors in budget projections would have several effects. At the macro level, it would make it harder to hit a planned deficit target and would give the appearance of losing control over fiscal policy. But part of the reason for missing deficit targets is the feedback of the economy on the deficit, causing the deficit to rise when the economy underperforms. From this perspective, unexpected changes in the economy that produce shifts in deficit projections should not lead to Congressional responses, making the increased uncertainty associated with biennial budgeting less of a problem.

Increased errors in budget projections could be more of a problem at the micro level. Though errors caused by inaccurate assumptions tend to be partially offsetting in the aggregate, they are often large for individual programs. These errors may lead to pressure to consider supplemental appropriations or rescind funds for some activities.

Consider some of the effects of unanticipated changes in interest rates, which are among the most uncertain economic forecast variables. At the program level, a rise in interest rates deepens the subsidies granted by fixed-rate loan programs, thus increasing the demand for loans. If the Congress wanted *to* reduce the actual subsidies to the planned amounts, it would have to pass bills that increased the fixed rates. If the Congress had limited the programs through ceilings on spending, it would have to raise the ceiling if it wanted to provide the deeper subsidy to all applicants. A similar situation would occur for variable-rate loan programs when interest rates declined. Alternatively, the Congress could decide to accept these effects and not take any action, or it could design credit programs that automatically respond to changes in interest rates.

When prices increase unexpectedly, planned purchases of goods and services become more expensive. Under current budget procedures, increased costs would require supplementals for purchases of minimum quantities of necessary goods, such as fuel for the military. Price decreases, on the other hand, could leave agencies overfunded and able to buy more than the Congress intended, which might lead the Congress and the President to consider rescissions.

Not all accounts are sensitive to these and similar uncertainties. Many accounts are for pay and benefits and are very stable. In addition, there are a number of procedures that could allow the Congress to cope with the increased uncertainty of a two-year budget period. The Congress could decide not to respond to minor changes in economic conditions with legislation, and it could automatically adjust the budget resolution for these changes. Pro forma appropriations for appropriated entitlements (such as Medicaid) and for other programs such as the Commodity Credit Corporation could be converted into permanent appropriations. Price variability could be dealt with through new methods of contracting and budgeting for inflation.[17] A single supplemental could be scheduled for the off-year with rules that would prevent funding for programs not previously authorized.

Other proposals for reducing uncertainty could effectively eliminate some of the potential gains from biennial budgeting. One example would be the practice of simultaneously providing two separate years of appropriations, each with one-year availability. Because the Congress could rescind the second year of funding before it would be obligated, contractors would still charge a premium to compensate for this risk. This would prevent agencies from purchasing goods and services in quantities large enough to minimize prices.[18]

Maintain the Influence of the Congress on Policy

One trade-off offered by biennial budgeting is that the Congress would replace annual appropriations with more program planning and oversight. How would this change affect the ability of the Congress to properly influence policy? Proponents of biennial budgeting claim that this change in activities would uncover problems not currently detected in appropriation reviews, allowing the Congress to address them. Opponents counter that these benefits would not offset the loss of influence that would result from forgoing the opportunity to make budget allocations annually.

This debate is not about the value of routine annual interactions between the Congress and the President, for it is generally agreed that annual interactions promote cooperation between the two branches.[19] Cooperation has two components – trust by the Congress that the Executive Branch will implement its directives, and respect by the Executive Branch for the Congress's right to make these directives. The debate is instead about which types of annual interactions promote the most trust and respect, and thus maintain the influence of the Congress on policy.

Throughout its history, the Congress has resolved this issue by following an annual process of making allocations. One way that annual appropriations increase its leverage over the Executive Branch is in providing vehicles for policy riders. Policy riders become starting points for negotiations between the branches because of the "must-pass" character of appropriation bills – if these bills are not enacted, government agencies that lack spending authority must shut down. Even though the Congress often shares the blame for shutdowns, potential shutdowns place pressure on the Executive Branch to negotiate. In the absence of "must-pass" legislative vehicles, the Executive Branch would usually not negotiate on policy disputes to the degree that it does now.[20]

Annual appropriations also encourage the Executive Branch to implement the budget in good faith. If agency expenditures are inconsistent with Congressional intent, the Congress may then influence the Administration by withholding approval of its pending appropriation requests (though the Administration may doubt the credibility of such threats). Under the split-sessions model of biennial budgeting, the Congress would instead have to rely on oversight to monitor agency spending and to prod the Executive Branch to spend appropriated funds properly. But oversight can be ineffective when the Administration lacks concern about violating Congressional intent.[21]

The Congress has also used annual authorizations, which often establish spending floors and ceilings in great detail, to order compliance with its goals.[22] The rules of the Congress establish points of order against unauthorized appropriations, making authorizations priority legislation. Exceptions to these rules, however, are increasingly common. Exceptions are important because as long as appropriations are enacted, funds may be obligated by agencies, regardless of whether annual authorizations have been enacted. These exceptions and the willingness of President Reagan to veto authorizations have led to reductions in the rates of consideration and passage of annual authorizations in the 1980s, which has lessened the utility of annual authorizations for exercising Congressional influence.

The desire for flexibility is another reason for annually considering budget resolutions and making appropriations. Many consider annual budgeting to be the only responsible course of action with large deficits, because it allows recurring efforts to find political compromises on deficit reductions. The deficits have caused continued use of the reconciliation procedure to retrench spending in mandatory programs. Flexibility is also the reason why almost all salary and expense accounts are appropriated annually, even though they are the least complex and most predictable accounts of all.[23]

Proponents of biennial budgeting do not agree that these traditional methods of preserving influence and flexibility are as effective as generally thought. They argue that the Congress is organizationally limited in what it can do each year. They also note that the Congress has decided that annual allocations are unnecessary or counterproductive for many programs. The Congress does not vote annually to allocate funds to Social Security and some other entitlement programs, for example, because there is a consensus that these programs are longterm commitments. Nor does it vote appropriations annually to pay interest on the national debt or to fund a multiyear ship contract in annual stages. As a result of similar decisions for other programs, only a fourth of appropriations have been annual appropriations of one-year availability.

Also disturbing to proponents of biennial budgeting are the costs of annual budgeting to those who carry out policies. Annual budgeting is said to encourage wmicromanagement" – the assumption by the Congress of what are typically the responsibilities of program managers. Many agencies claim that line-item directives in annual appropriation and authorization bills would reduce the number of directives. If, however, the Congress places directives in bills because it fears that agencies will spend money inappropriately, biennial authorizations and appropriations could contain even more "micromanagement" provisions.

Statements that agency officials will save time and paperwork because they will not have to prepare and justify their budgets each year may be overly optimistic as well. One presumption of biennial budgeting is that the Congress will do more oversight. For the Congress to conduct performance reviews, those doing the performing will presumably have to respond to the requests of the Congress. The format of agency presentations to the Congress might well change, as may the officials who do presentations (line officials instead of budget officials), but agencies' work loads will probably not decline if the Congress vigorously conducts oversight.

Another purported benefit from biennial budgeting has been that it would give grantees—usually state and local governments – earlier knowledge of available funding and allow them to spend money more efficiently. Although this idea has merit, the extent of the benefit would be limited. In the first place, many grants are already predictable. Nearly two-thirds of grants are mandatory, and most mandatory grants are allocated by formulas. An additional 6 percent of grants, in the education area, are forward funded. Forward funding allows an agency to make grants in one fiscal year for the succeeding fiscal year.[24] To the extent that reconciliation or rescissions do not change these budgeted amounts, grantees already know with some certainty the funds that they will receive. For the remaining grants, the benefit of earlier knowledge from biennial budgeting would apply to only the second year of the biennium, because the grants for the first year of the biennium would be made shortly after the adoption of the budget.[25]

Thus, though the efficiency of budgeting would not increase dramatically under a biennial format, some improvement is likely. This biennial approach could be enhanced by a budgetwide reexamination of the periodicity of budget reviews at the program and project level. Programs that are funded by annual, one-year availability appropriations have traditionally borne the brunt of budget reductions, a tradition that was carried on by the Balanced Budget Act's sequester procedures. Agencies often claim that reductions in these appropriations are of the penny-wise, pound-foolish variety. They commonly cite their failure to make needed investments because appropriations are cut, even though the investments would reduce operating and total costs in the long run. This effect, and the more general risk of budget reductions, encourages agencies to convert their programs into the form of mandatory spending. In the long run, this locks in spending and leads to less flexibility in the total budget.

An alternative means of increasing flexibility would be to strengthen controls on mandatory spending, which would require improved recognition of the full costs of potential multiyear commitments when considering whether to enter into them. It would also require that mandatory spending be reauthorized periodically and subjected to a tough reconciliation procedure. Biennial budgeting might contribute to this approach by shifting the perspective from one year to two, thereby reducing the fixation on one-year spending cuts and making false savings from effective date changes less attractive. With the resulting increase in flexibility in these accounts, the selective biennial approach suggested by the Balanced Budget Reaffirmation Act could be followed with fewer grounds for concern about the loss of flexibility. For example, multiyear authorizations and appropriations could be made for stages of long-term procurements, rather than providing appropriations for variable numbers of units in each [26]

End Notes for Section I

[1] Multiyear appropriations are available for spending over several specified years; no-year appropriations are available until spent; and advance appropriations are available beginning in the fiscal year succeeding the year for which the appropriation bill is passed. Data compiled from OMB tapes by Allen Schick, *Crisis in the Budget Process* (Washington, D.C.: American Enterprise Institute, 1986), pp. 47-49.

[2] CBO data show that although 15.2 percent of nondefense discretionary appropriations were subject to annual authorization, only 3.2 percent were authorized in 1987. Only 10 annual

authorization bills were enacted out of the 19 bills that are routinely considered on an annual basis.

[3] This provision has never been successfully carried out.

[4] A list of biennial budgeting bills from 1977 to the present is contained in the appendix of Michael D. Margeson and James Saturno, "Congressional Approaches to Biennial Budgeting" (Congressional Research Service, July 27, 1987), pp. 19-21.

[5] See Senate Committee on Governmental Affairs, "Review of the Congressional Budget and Impoundment Control Act of 1974" (October 6 and 29, 1981) and "Budget Reform Act of 1982" (August 19, 1982); House Budget Committee, "Budget Process Review" (September 14, 1982); and Senate Budget Committee, "Proposed Improvements in the Congressional Budget Act of 1974" (September 14, 16, 21, and 23, 1982).

[6] Task Force on the Budget Process of the House Committee on Rules, "Recommendations to Improve the Congressional Budget Process" (May 1984), p. 24.

[7] See House Committee on Rules, "Congressional Budget Act Amendments of 1984," Report 98-1152 (October 1984); and Robert A. Keith, "Changes in the Congressional Budget Process Made by the 1985 Balanced Budget Act (P.L. 99-177)" (Congressional Research Service, May 23, 1986).

[8] See *Congressional Record,* July 31, 1985, S10557-10562.

[9] In a recent survey by the Center for Responsive Politics, 86 percent of a sample of 113 House Members and Senators supported biennial appropriations. See *Congress Speaks: A Survey of the 100th Congress* (Washington, D.C.: 1988), p. 34; see also Jonathan Rauch, "Biennial Budgeting Taking Root," *National Journal,* vol. 18 (September 27, 1986), pp. 2318-2319; and Alice M. Rivlin, "Taming the Economic Policy Monster," *New York Times,* January 18,1987, p. F2.

[10] Continuing resolutions provide funding for agencies that have not received appropriations in regular appropriation bills. Traditionally enacted for short periods after the beginning of the fiscal year for one or several agencies, continuing resolutions have been enacted in recent years for many agencies and for the balance of the fiscal year.

[11] *Congressional Record, May* 6, 1987, S6010-6013.

[12] See Edward Davis and Robert Keith, "Debt-Limit Increase and 1985 Balanced Budget Act Reaffirmation: Summary of Public Law 100-119 (H.J. Res. 324)" (Congressional Research Service, October 29, 1987).

[13] S.1563, described in the *Congressional Record,* July 29, 1987, S10861-10862.

End Notes for Section II

[1] Introductory statements in support of these bills can be found in the *Congressional Record,* January 6, 1987, H23-26 for H.R. 22; January 12, 1987, S601-609 for S. 286; and January 29, 1987, S1321-1333 for S. 416.

[2] S. 416 also permits amendment of the first budget resolution only if two-thirds of both the House and the Senate agree, and establishes a point of order against violating the Balanced Budget Act's maximum deficit amount for each year in the biennium. It requires reporting of all 13 regular appropriation bills before considering an appropriation bill on the floor, extends CBO cost estimates to six years, and mandates that the account structure of the President's budget be used in all Congressional budget actions.

[3] S. 286 requires that the account structure of the President's budget be used in all Congressional budget actions, requires committees to file oversight reports by the beginning of the biennium, and establishes an automatic continuing resolution at the previous rate of operations. In addition, it prohibits reconciliation until after the second resolution and limits reconciliation to changes in entitlement authority, revenues, and the debt limit.

End Notes for Section III

[1] Sources on biennial budgeting in the states are Barbara Yondorf, "Annual Versus Biennial Budgeting: The Arguments, The Evidence" (National Conference of State Legislatures, January 26, 1987); Charles W. Wiggins and Keith E. Hamm, "Annual Versus Biennial Budgeting?" (Texas A&M University, August 1984); and General Accounting Office, "Current Status and Recent Trends of State Biennial and Annual Budgeting" (July 15, 1987), "Biennial Budgeting. Summary of the Major Issues" (April 17, 1984), and "Biennial Budgeting: The State Examples" (December 23, 1982).

[2] Comprehensive information on international budgetary practices has not been compiled. The information in this section was drawn from various articles in *Public Budgeting and Finance* from 1982 to the present; from discussions with country specialists at the State Department, the Federal Reserve, and the International Monetary Fund; and from A. Premchand, *Government Budgeting and Expenditure Controls* (Washington, D.C.: International Monetary Fund, 1983), pp. 137-143.

3 The mean population difference is 1.4 million, compared with a mean state population of 4.8 million. The median population difference is 0.6 million, compared with a median state population of 3.3 million. Figures are based on 1985 U.S. Census data.

End Notes for Section IV

[1] Similar rules might profitably be applied to supplementals and rescissions under annual budgeting. Pay raises, now provided in supplemental bills, could easily be incorporated into the regular appropriation bills. Section 207 of the Balanced Budget and Emergency Deficit Control Reaffirmation Act of 1987 prohibited the President from repeatedly proposing similar rescission requests.

[2] Joel D. Aberbach, *Keeping a Watchful Eye: The Politics of Congressional Oversight* (Washington, D.C.: Brookings Institution, forthcoming).

[3] See also Joel D. Aberbach, "The Congressional Committee Intelligence System: Information, Oversight, and Change," *Congress and the Presidency,* vol. 14 (Spring 1987), pp. 51-76. Another useful source on oversight is the *Congressional Oversight Manual,* prepared by the Congressional Research Service, February 1984.

[4] Discussions of the historical relationships between the authorization and appropriation processes are available in Allen Schick, "Legislation, Appropriations, and Budgets: The Development of Spending Decision-Making in Congress" (Congressional Research Service, May 1984); Louis Fisher, "The Authorization-Appropriations Process: Formal Rules and Informal Practices" (Congressional Research Service, August 1, 1979); and W. Thomas

Wander, "Patterns of Change in the Congressional Budget Process, 1865-1974," *Congress and the Presidency, vol.* 9 (Autumn 1982), pp. 2349.

[5] That many authorizations are budgetary in nature suggests that enacting advance authorizations would not limit off-year activities to nonbudgetary ones. On the various approaches to multiyear and advance authorizations, see Stanley I. Bach, "Approaches to the Issue of Unauthorized Appropriations" (Congressional Research Service, July 31, 1978).

[6] The Congress has infrequently adopted major committee reforms to reduce overlaps. Landmark reforms were the Legislative Reorganization Act of 1946 and the Senate's acceptance in 1977 of the recommendations of the Stevenson Committee (the Temporary Select Committee to Study the Senate Committee System). In the 100th Congress, S. Res. 260, introduced by Senators Kassebaum and Inouye, would combine the appropriation and authorization processes. It would abolish the Senate Budget Committee and transfer its responsibilities to a "Committee on National Priorities," which would be constituted as a supercommittee of leaders of the other committees.

[7] Useful sources on committee reform are Roger H. Davidson and Walter J. Oleszek, *Congress Against Itself* (Bloomington, Indiana: Indiana University Press, 1977); and Congressional Quarterly Inc., "The Committee System," *Guide to the Congress,* 3rd ed. (Washington, D.C.: CQ Press, 1982), particularly pp. 466-476.

[8] A useful analysis of omnibus budgeting is provided by Allen Schick, "The Whole and the Parts: Piecemeal and Integrated Approaches to Congressional Budgeting," House Budget Committee, Serial CP-3 (February 1987).

[9] As evidence that an omnibus procedure would not work, opponents point to the 1950 omnibus appropriation bill. The bill was approved five weeks after the beginning of the fiscal year, but two calendar months before the passage of the last appropriation bill in the previous year. The omnibus procedure was discarded by the House and Senate Appropriations Committees the next year, in part because of opposition from the House leadership. See Dalmas H. Nelson, "The Omnibus Appropriations Act of 1950," *The Journal of Politics* vol. 15 (May 1953), pp. 274-288; and George B. Galloway, "Consolidated Appropriation Bill," Legislative Reference Service, Library of Congress (October 15, 1953).

[10] This figure was calculated from data in General Accounting Office, "Funding Gaps Jeopardize Federal Government Operations" (March 3, 1981).

[11] On the relationship between elections and changes in budget allocations, see D. Roderick Kiewiet and Mathew D. McCubbins, "Congressional Appropriations and the Electoral Connection," *Journal of Politics,* vol. 47 (February 1985), pp. 59-82.

[12] See pp. 85-86 and 94.

[13] See also David C. Grinnel, "Implications of Uncertainty in Economic Forecasting Under Gramm-Rudman-Hollings: Options for Congressional Response" (Congressional Research Service, August 8, 1986).

[14] CBO, *The Economic and Budget Outlook: Fiscal Years 1989-1993,* (February 1988).

[15] On October 15,1988, OMB will determine the actual savings required to meet the deficit reduction targets.

[16] Policy changes in the budget year distort the previous year's out-year baseline estimates for programs, making an estimate of the change in technical projection errors unreliable.

[17] See Congressional Budget *Office, Budgeting for Defense Inflation* (January 1986).

[18] See Congressional Budget Office, *Assessing the Effectiveness of Milestone Budgeting* (July 1987), for a discussion of these and related topics.

[19] For a convincing presentation of the argument that cooperation is encouraged by frequent interaction, see Robert Axelrod, *The Evolution of Cooperation* (New York: Basic Books, 1984). On annuality and cooperation in budgeting, see Aaron Wildaysky, *The Politics of the Budgetary Process,* 4th ed. (Boston: Little, Brown, 1984); and Richard F. Fenno, Jr., *The Power of the Purse* (Boston: Little, Brown, 1966).

[20] On the value of riders, see Roger H. Davidson, "Procedures and Politics in Congress," in Gilbert Y. Steiner, ed., *The Abortion Dispute and the American System* (Washington, D.C.: Brookings Institution, 1983), pp. 30-46, especially p. 45; and Allen Schick, "Politics through Law: Congressional Limitations on Executive Discretion," in Anthony King, *Both Ends of the Avenue* (Washington, D.C.: American Enterprise Institute, 1983), pp. 154-184, especially pp. 171-173.

[21] See James L. Sundquist, *The Decline and Resurgence of Congress* (Washington, D.C.: Brookings Institution, 1981), Chapter 11. See also Louis Fisher, *Presidential Spending Power* (Princeton: Princeton University Press, 1975); chapter 4 provides examples of reprogramming procedures that had not been honored by agencies, leading committees to restate and tighten procedures or to take punitive actions.

[22] Louis Fisher, "Annual Authorizations: Durable Roadblocks to Biennial Budgeting," *Public Budgeting and Finance,* vol. 3 (Spring 1983), pp. 23-40.

[23] The Congress acted in 1934,1946,1966,1970, and 1974 to repeal or study the repeal of permanent appropriations in order to increase flexibility. See Michael D. Margeson and James Saturno, "Congressional Approaches to Biennial Budgeting" (Congressional Research Service, July 27, 1987), p. 9.

[24] A number of other grant programs in the education area are authorized to receive advance appropriations, but these appropriations have not been provided.

[25] Section 502(c) of the Congressional Budget Act mandated two reports on advance budgeting, published as Congressional Budget Office, "Advance Budgeting: A Report to the Congress" (March 1977); and Office of Management and Budget, "A Study of the Advisability of Submitting the President's Budget and Enacting Budget Authority in Advance of the Current Timetable" (1977). The CBO report cautiously supported reauthorization of grant programs a year before the expiration of the existing authorization. The report also outlined a process for considering which programs could be appropriated on a two-year schedule. The OMB report concluded that advance funding would cause too great a loss of flexibility in the budget year, and proposed the alternative of including in the budget "target amounts" of planned grant appropriations for two out-years.

[26] See Congressional Budget *Office, Assessing the Effectiveness of Milestone Budgeting.*

In: Biennial Budgeting
Editor: Carolyn Douglas

ISBN: 978-1-63482-673-0

Chapter 3

INTRODUCTION TO THE FEDERAL BUDGET PROCESS*

Bill Heniff, Megan Suzanne Lynch and Jessica Tollestrup

SUMMARY

Budgeting for the federal government is an enormously complex process. It entails dozens of subprocesses, countless rules and procedures, the efforts of tens of thousands of staff persons in the executive and legislative branches, millions of work hours each year, and the active participation of the President and congressional leaders, as well as other members of Congress and executive officials.

The enforcement of budgetary decisions involves a complex web of procedures that encompasses both congressional and executive actions. In the last four decades or so, these procedures have been rooted principally in two statutes—the Congressional Budget Act of 1974 and the Balanced Budget and Emergency Deficit Control Act of 1985. The 1974 act established a congressional budget process in which budget policies are enforced by Congress during the consideration of individual measures. The 1985 act embodies additional statutory enforcement procedures, substantially modified

* This is an edited, reformatted and augmented version of the Congressional Research Service Publication, CRS Report for Congress 98-721, dated December 3, 2012.

in 1990 and 1997, that have been used by the executive to enforce budget policies after the end of a congressional session. The 1997 iteration of these enforcement procedures were set aside in the latter years of their existence and effectively expired toward the end of the 107th Congress. Efforts to renew them in the 108th through 110th Congresses were not successful. In the 111th Congress, the pay-as-you-go procedures affecting direct spending and revenue legislation were restored in a modified version by the Statutory Pay-As-You-Go Act of 2010. More recently, in the 112th Congress, statutory limits on discretionary spending and a new automatic process to reduce spending were established by the Budget Control Act of 2011.

The President's budget is required by law to be submitted to Congress early in the legislative session. While the budget is only a request to Congress, the power to formulate and submit the budget is a vital tool in the President's direction of the executive branch and of national policy. The President's proposals often influence congressional revenue and spending decisions, though the extent of the influence varies from year to year and depends more on political and fiscal conditions than on the legal status of the budget.

The Congressional Budget Act of 1974 establishes the congressional budget process as the means by which Congress coordinates the various budget-related actions (such as the consideration of appropriations and revenue measures) taken by it during the course of the year. The process is centered on an annual concurrent resolution on the budget that sets aggregate budget policies and functional spending priorities for at least the next five fiscal years. Because a concurrent resolution is not a law—it cannot be signed or vetoed by the President—the budget resolution does not have statutory effect; no money can be raised or spent pursuant to it. Revenue and spending amounts set in the budget resolution establish the basis for the enforcement of congressional budget policies through points of order.

Congress implements budget resolution policies through action on individual revenue and debt- limit measures, annual appropriations acts, and direct spending legislation. In some years, Congress considers reconciliation legislation pursuant to reconciliation instructions in the budget resolution. Reconciliation legislation is used mainly to bring existing revenue and direct spending laws into conformity with budget resolution policies. Initially, reconciliation was a major tool for deficit reduction; in later years, reconciliation was used mainly to reduce revenues.

THE EVOLUTION OF FEDERAL BUDGETING

The "power of the purse" is a legislative power. The Constitution lists the power to lay and collect taxes and the power to borrow as powers of Congress; further, it provides that funds may be drawn from the Treasury only pursuant to appropriations made by law. The Constitution does not state how these legislative powers are to be exercised, nor does it expressly provide for the President to have a role in the management of the nation's finances.

During the nation's early years, the House and Senate devised procedures for the enactment of spending and revenue legislation. As these procedures evolved during the 19th century and the first decades of the 20th century, they led to highly fragmented legislative actions. In the course of each session, Congress passed many separate appropriations bills and other measures affecting the financial condition of the federal government. Neither the Constitution nor the procedures adopted by the House and Senate provided for a budget system—that is, for a coordinated set of actions covering all federal spending and revenues. As long as the federal government was small and its spending and revenues were stable, such a budget system was not considered necessary.

Early in the 20th century, the incessant rise in federal spending and the recurrence of deficits (spending exceeded revenues in half of the 20 years preceding FY1920) led Congress to seek a more coordinated means of making financial decisions. The key legislation was the Budget and Accounting Act of 1921, which established the executive budget process.

The 1921 act did not directly alter the procedures by which Congress makes revenue and spending decisions. The main impact was in the executive branch. The President was required to submit his budget recommendations to Congress each year, and the Bureau of the Budget— renamed the Office of Management and Budget (OMB) in 1970—was created to assist him in carrying out his budgetary responsibilities. Congress, it was expected, would be able to coordinate its revenue and spending decisions if it received comprehensive budget recommendations from the President. In line with this expectation, the House and Senate changed their rules to consolidate the jurisdiction of the Appropriations Committees over spending. The 1921 act also established the General Accounting Office (GAO), headed by the Comptroller General, and made it the principal auditing arm of the federal government. (The GAO recently was renamed the Government Accountability Office.) The 1921 act, as amended, remains the statutory basis for the presidential budget system.

After World War II, the belief that the presidential budget sufficed to maintain fiscal control gave way to the view that Congress needed its own budget process. Some members of Congress feared that dependence on the executive budget had bolstered the President's fiscal powers at the expense of Congress's; others felt that as long as its financial decisions were fragmented, Congress could not effectively control expenditures.

The Congressional Budget and Impoundment Control Act of 1974 established a congressional budget process centered on a concurrent resolution on the budget, scheduled for adoption prior to legislative consideration of revenue or spending bills. The congressional budget process initiated in the 1970s did not replace the preexisting revenue and spending processes. Instead, it provided an overall legislative framework within which the many separate measures affecting the budget would be considered. The central purpose of the budget process established by the 1974 act is to coordinate the various revenue and spending decisions which are made in separate revenue, appropriations, and other budgetary measures. To assist Congress in making budget decisions, the 1974 act established the Congressional Budget Office (CBO) and directed it to provide data on and analyses of the federal budget.

During the years that the congressional budget process has been in operation, its procedures have been adapted by Congress to changing circumstances. Following a decade of experience with the 1974 Congressional Budget Act, Congress made further changes in the budget process by enacting the Balanced Budget and Emergency Deficit Control Act of 1985 (also known as the Gramm-Rudman-Hollings Act), the Budget Enforcement Act of 1990 (BEA), the Line Item Veto Act in 1996, the Budget Enforcement Act of 1997, the Statutory Pay-As-You-Go Act of 2010, and the Budget Control Act of 2011, among other laws.

The 1985 act prescribed declining deficit targets intended to achieve balance in FY1991; the targets were enforced by sequestration, a process involving automatic, across-the-board cuts in nonexempt spending programs if the targets were expected to be exceeded. The 1990 act replaced the deficit targets with caps on discretionary spending and a pay-as-you-go (PAYGO) requirement for revenue and direct spending legislation; sequestration was retained as the means of enforcing the two new mechanisms. The 1996 act authorized the President to cancel discretionary spending in appropriation acts, as well as new direct spending and limited tax benefits in other legislation, subject to expedited legislative procedures by which Congress could overturn the cancellations. (The Supreme Court struck down the Line Item Veto Act in June 1998 as unconstitutional.) The 1997 act extended the BEA procedures for several more years. Without a consensus on extending the control mechanisms under the BEA, however, they expired at the end of FY2002. The Statutory Pay-As-You-Go Act of 2010 restored a modified version of the PAYGO requirement for direct spending and revenue legislation. More recently, as part of an agreement to increase the statutory limit on the public debt, the Budget Control Act of 2011 restored statutory limits on discretionary spending for each fiscal year through FY2021 and established an automatic process to reduce spending if subsequent legislation reducing the deficit by at least $1.2 trillion was not enacted, with spending reductions beginning in January 2013.

BASIC CONCEPTS OF FEDERAL BUDGETING

The federal budget is a compilation of numbers about the revenues, spending, and borrowing and debt of the government. Revenues come largely from taxes, but stem from other sources as well (such as duties, fines, licenses, and gifts). Spending involves such concepts as budget authority, obligations, outlays, and offsetting collections. The numbers are computed according to rules and conventions that have accumulated over the years; they do not always conform to the way revenues and spending are accounted for in other processes.

Budget Authority and Outlays

When Congress appropriates money, it provides *budget authority*, that is, authority to enter into obligations. Budget authority also may be provided in legislation that does not go through the appropriations process (*direct spending* legislation). The key congressional spending decisions relate to the obligations that agencies are authorized to incur during a fiscal year, not to the outlays made during the year. (*Obligations* occur when agencies enter into contracts, submit purchase orders, employ personnel, and so forth; *outlays* occur when obligations are liquidated, primarily through the issuance of checks, electronic fund transfers, or the disbursement of cash.)

The provision of budget authority is the key point at which Congress exercises control over federal spending, although the outlay level often receives greater public attention because of its bearing on the deficit. Congress does not directly control outlays; each year's outlays derive in part from new budget authority and in part from "carryover" budget authority provided in prior years. For example, President Barack Obama's initial budget submission for FY2013 estimated that outlays would total $3,803 billion for that year. Approximately $2,833 billion of this amount was estimated to come from new budget authority for the fiscal year, while the remainder ($970 billion) was estimated to come from budget authority enacted in prior years.

The relation of budget authority to outlays varies from program to program and depends on *spendout rates*, the rates at which funds provided by Congress are obligated and payments disbursed. In a program with a high spendout rate, most new budget authority is expended during the fiscal year; if the spendout rate is low, however, most of the outlays occur in later years. Regardless of the spendout rate, the outlays in the budget are merely estimates of the amounts that will be disbursed during the year. If payments turn out to be higher than the budget estimate, outlays will be above the budgeted level. The President and Congress control outlays indirectly by deciding on the amount of budget authority to be provided or by limiting the amount of obligations to be incurred.

Certain receipts of the federal government are accounted for as "offsets" against outlays rather than as revenues. Various fees collected by government agencies are deducted from outlays; similarly, income from the sale of certain assets are treated as *offsetting receipts*. Most such receipts are offsets against the outlays of the agencies that collect the money, but in the case of offshore oil leases and certain other activities, the revenues are deducted from the total outlays of the government.

Scope of the Budget

The budget consists of two main groups of funds: *federal funds and trust funds*. Federal funds— which comprise mainly the general fund—largely derive from the general exercise of the taxing power and general borrowing and for the most part are not earmarked by law to any specific program or agency. One component of federal funds, called special funds, is earmarked as to source and purpose. The use of federal funds is determined largely by appropriations acts.

Trust funds are established, under the terms of statutes that designate them as trust funds, to account for funds earmarked by specific sources and purposes. The Social Security funds are the largest of the trust funds; revenues are collected under a Social Security payroll tax and are used to pay for Social Security benefits and related purposes. The *unified budget* includes both the federal funds and the trust funds. The balances in the trust funds are borrowed by the federal government; they are counted, therefore, in the federal debt. Because these balances offset a budget deficit but are included in the federal debt, the annual increase in the debt invariably exceeds the amount of the budget deficit. For the same reason, it is possible for the federal debt to rise when the federal government has a budget surplus.

Capital and operating expenses are not segregated in the budget. Hence, monies paid for the operations of government agencies as well as for the acquisition of long-life assets (such as buildings, roads, and weapons systems) are reported as budget outlays. Proposals have been made from time to time to divide the budget into capital and operating accounts. While these proposals have not been adopted, the budget provides information showing the investment and operating outlays of the government.

The budget totals do not include all the financial transactions of the federal government. The main exclusions fall into two categories—off-budget entities and government-sponsored enterprises. In addition, the budget includes direct and guaranteed loans on the basis of the accounting rules established by the Federal Credit Reform Act of 1990, which are discussed below.

Off-budget entities are excluded by law from the budget totals. The receipts and disbursements of the Social Security trust funds (the Old-Age and Survivors Insurance Fund and the Disability Insurance Fund), as well as spending for the Postal Service Fund, are excluded from the budget totals. These transactions are shown separately in the budget. Thus, the budget now reports two deficit or surplus amounts—one excluding the Social Security trust funds and the Postal Service Fund, and the other (on a unified basis) including these entities. The latter is the main focus of discussion in both the President's budget and the congressional budget process.

The transactions of government-owned corporations (excluding the Postal Service), as well as revolving funds, are included in the budget on a net basis. That is, the amount shown in the budget is the difference between receipts and outlays, not the total activity of the enterprise or revolving fund. If, for example, a revolving fund has annual income of $150 million and disbursements of $200 million, the budget would report $50 million as net outlays.

Government-sponsored enterprises (GSEs) historically have been excluded from the budget because they were deemed to be private rather than public entities. The federal government did not own any equity in these enterprises, most of which received their financing from private sources.

Although they were established by the federal government, their budgets were not reviewed by the President or Congress in the same manner as other programs. Most of these enterprises engaged in credit activities. They borrowed funds in capital markets and lent money to homeowners, farmers, and others. In total, these enterprises had assets and liabilities measured in trillions of dollars. Financial statements of the government-sponsored enterprises were published in the President's budget.

Although some GSEs continue to operate on this basis, the economic downturn and credit instability that occurred in 2008 fundamentally changed the status of two GSEs that play a significant role in the home mortgage market, Fannie Mae and Freddie Mac. In September of 2008, the Federal Housing Finance Agency (FHFA) placed the two entities in conservatorship, thereby subjecting them to control by the Federal Government until the conservatorship eventually is brought to an end.

Deficit Reduction and the Rules of Congressional Budgeting

Between the early 1980s and the late 1990s, annual consideration of the budget was dominated by concern about the budget deficit. In the mid-1980s, the deficit exceeded $150 billion and amounted to about 6% of GDP at one point. In the early 1990s, the deficit approached the $300 billion level. Following four years of surpluses (FY1998-FY2001), the budget returned to deficit for FY2002. Current budget projections show sizeable deficits persisting over the coming years.

The size of the deficit depends on how it is measured. The unified budget deficit combines all on- budget federal funds and trust funds with the off-budget entities (the Social Security trust funds and the Postal Service Fund). The unified budget deficit generally is regarded as the most comprehensive measure of the impact of the budget on the economy. A narrower measure of the deficit is derived by excluding the Social Security trust funds from the totals. This exclusion is mandated by law, although Social Security is counted in the budget in reports on the deficit. Excluding Social Security from computations of the deficit or surplus results in higher deficit or lower surplus figures.

Regardless of the measure used, it is evident that the deficit was unusually high for an extended period of time. The chronic deficits of the 1980s prompted Congress to enact the Balanced Budget and Emergency Deficit Control Act of 1985. The 1985 act established deficit targets for each year through FY1991, when the budget was to be balanced, and a sequestration process under which budgetary resources would be canceled automatically (through largely across-the- board spending cuts) if the estimated deficit exceeded the amount allowed under the act.

Even with the targets, the actual deficit for the covered years was above the targeted level. Failure to achieve the deficit targets, and other problems, led Congress to revise the process in the Budget Enforcement Act (BEA) of 1990. Sequestration procedures were retained, but the fixed deficit targets were replaced by adjustable ones (which expired at the end of FY1995), adjustable limits were imposed on discretionary spending, and a pay-as-you-go (PAYGO) process was established for revenues and direct spending. The discretionary spending limits and PAYGO process were extended (through FY1998) by the Omnibus Budget Reconciliation of 1993 and again (through FY2002) by the BEA of 1997.

Under the discretionary spending limits, different categories of discretionary spending were used for different periods. Under the 1997 changes, discretionary spending limits applied separately to defense and nondefense spending for FY1998-FY1999 and to violent crime reduction spending for FY1998-FY2000; for the remaining fiscal years, the 1997 changes merged all discretionary spending into a single, general purpose category. In 1998, as part of the Transportation Equity Act for the 21st Century, Congress added separate categories for highway and mass transit spending. Finally, in 2000, Congress added a category for conservation spending; unlike the other categories, the conservation spending category had six subcategories.

The PAYGO process under the BEA required that the budgetary impact of revenue and direct spending legislation be recorded on a multiyear "PAYGO scorecard," and that in the net any such legislation not yield a negative balance for the upcoming fiscal year. Legislation reducing revenues or increasing direct spending for a fiscal year had to be offset (in the same or other legislation) by revenue increases or reductions in direct spending for that fiscal year so that the applicable balance on the PAYGO scorecard remained at or above zero.

Under the BEA procedures, violations of the discretionary spending limits or the PAYGO requirement were to be enforced by sequestration. However, sequestration was not used for more than a decade, either because Congress and the President enacted budgetary legislation consistent with the discretionary spending limits and PAYGO requirement, or, during the latter years under the BEA, effectively waived these enforcement requirements.

The BEA enforcement procedures effectively expired toward the end of the 107th Congress. As budget deficits persisted through the last decade, proposals to restore the BEA statutory procedures had been made from time to time by members of Congress and the President, but none of the proposals were enacted until 2010. The Statutory Pay-As-You-Go Act of 2010 (P.L. 111-139) restored in statute a modified version of the PAYGO requirement for direct spending and revenue legislation.[1] Subsequently, in 2011, the Budget Control Act (P.L. 112-25) established statutory limits on discretionary spending for each year through FY2021.

Like the previous statutory PAYGO requirement under the BEA, the new statutory PAYGO requirement is intended to discourage or prevent Congress from taking certain legislative action that would increase the on-budget deficit. It generally requires that legislation affecting direct spending or revenues not increase the deficit over a six-year period and an 11-year period. Likewise, the current statutory discretionary caps established under the Budget Control Act are similar to those under the BEA. The limits essentially cap the amount of spending provided and controlled through the annual appropriations process each year, with upward adjustments to these limits permitted for certain purposes, such as for Overseas Contingency Operations.

The statutory PAYGO requirement and the statutory discretionary spending limits are enforced by sequestration—the cancellation of budgetary resources provided by laws affecting direct spending. Further information on sequestration is provided in the "The Sequestration Process" section, below.

During the 1990s to the present, the Senate has supplemented the statutory PAYGO requirement with a special PAYGO rule included in annual budget resolutions; following the expiration of the BEA procedures, the Senate extended its PAYGO rule (currently through FY2017). The Senate PAYGO rule currently prohibits the consideration of any legislation that proposes changes in direct spending or revenue that increase the deficit over six-year and 11-year time periods (including the current fiscal year). The House adopted its own PAYGO rule for the first time at the beginning of the 110th Congress. At the beginning of the 112th Congress, however, the House modified this rule, renaming it CutGo, or cut-as-you-go, to prohibit the consideration of any legislation that would have the net effect of increasing direct spending over the same two time periods.

BUDGETING FOR DISCRETIONARY AND DIRECT SPENDING

The distinction drawn by the BEA and the congressional budget process between discretionary spending (which is controlled through the annual appropriations process) and direct spending (which is provided outside of the annual appropriations process) recognized that the federal government has somewhat different, though overlapping, means of dealing with these two types of spending. One set of procedures pertained to discretionary spending, another to direct spending.

Most of the direct spending subject to the PAYGO process under the BEA involved entitlement programs; the rest consisted of other forms of mandatory spending provided through authorizing legislation and interest payments. In fact, entitlements now account for about half of total federal spending (all direct spending, including net interest, accounts for about 60% of the total). The impressive feature of this trend is that most of the growth in spending and in the number of recipients has been built into existing law; for the most part, it has not been the result of new legislation.

The procedures for discretionary and direct spending converge at two critical points in federal budgeting: formulation of the President's budget and formulation of the congressional budget resolution. Both of these policy statements encompass discretionary and direct spending, but the procedures used in budgeting for these types of expenditure differ greatly. The distinctions have some notable exceptions. Some procedures associated with direct spending are applied to particular types of discretionary programs, and vice versa. Nevertheless, the generalizations presented here help to explain the complications of the budget process and explain how decisions are made.

(1) *Budgetary Impact of Authorizing Legislation.* An authorization for a discretionary spending program is only a license to enact an appropriation. The amount of budgetary resources available for spending is determined in annual appropriations acts. For direct spending programs (principally entitlements), on the other hand, the authorizing legislation either provides, or effectively mandates the appropriation of, budget authority. In those entitlement programs that are subject to annual appropriation, the Appropriations Committees have little or no discretion as to the amounts they provide.

(2) *Committees That Provide or Mandate Budget Authority.* The Appropriations Committees have jurisdiction and effective control over discretionary spending programs, while authorizing committees

effectively control direct spending programs (including those funded in annual appropriations acts). In fact, committee jurisdiction determines whether a program is classified as discretionary or direct spending. All spending under the effective control of the Appropriations Committees is discretionary; everything else is direct spending. Accordingly, when legislation establishes a program as discretionary or direct spending, it not only determines the character of spending but the locus of congressional committee control as well.

(3) *Frequency of Decision-Making*. Discretionary appropriations are, with few exceptions, made annually for the current or next fiscal year. Direct spending programs typically are established in permanent law that continues in effect until such time as it is revised or terminated by another law. The fact that many entitlements have annual appropriations does not diminish the permanence of the laws governing the amounts spent. It should be noted, however, that some direct spending programs, such as Medicare, have been subject to frequent legislative changes. The purpose of such legislation has been to modify existing law, not to provide annual funding.

(4) *Means of Enforcing the Budget Resolution*. The procedures used by Congress to enforce the policies set forth in the annual budget resolution differ somewhat for discretionary and direct spending programs. For both types of spending, Congress relies on allocations made under Section 302 of the 1974 Congressional Budget Act to ensure that spending legislation reported by House and Senate committees conforms to established budget policies. But although this procedure is effective in controlling new legislation—both annual appropriations measures and new entitlement legislation—it is not an effective control on the spending that results from existing laws. Hence, Congress relies on reconciliation procedures to enforce budget policies with respect to existing spending and revenue laws. Reconciliation is not currently applied to discretionary programs funded in annual appropriations measures.

(5) *Statutory Controls*. Discretionary programs have been subject to the spending limits set in the BEA. Direct spending has not been capped, but has operated under the PAYGO process, which required that direct spending and revenue legislation enacted for a fiscal year not cause the deficit to rise or the surplus to decrease. The lack of caps was due to the fact that most direct spending programs are open-

ended, with spending determined by eligibility rules and payment formulas in existing law rather than by new legislation.

Budget enforcement depends on timely information concerning the status of federal revenues and spending. When it acts on legislation, Congress must be informed of the estimated impact on future budgets. Measuring these impacts often is referred to as "scoring" or "scorekeeping." Scoring discretionary spending measures is a much simpler task than scoring direct spending and revenue legislation. In the latter case, scoring always is done in reference to baseline projections of future revenues and spending.

Most appropriations are for a definite amount and the budget authority is provided for a single fiscal year. The main task is to estimate the outlays that will derive in the next year and beyond from the budget authority provided in the appropriations bill. CBO and the Appropriations Committees base these estimates on outlay (or spendout) rates—the percentage of budget authority that is spent in each year. These outlay rates vary by account and are based on historical records. For example, if $1 billion is appropriated to an account which has a spendout rate of 80% in the first fiscal year that funds become available, the outlay estimate for that fiscal year will be $800 million; the remaining $200 million will become outlays in one or more subsequent years.

Scorekeeping is much more complex in enforcing budget rules, such as the PAYGO requirements, relating to direct spending and revenues. For one thing, unlike appropriations, revenue and direct spending legislation usually is open-ended; it does not specify the amount by which revenue or spending will be changed. For another, the impact of this type of legislation continues in future years. In enforcing the PAYGO requirements, Congress had to estimate the revenue gain or loss for the ensuing five years under the BEA, and for 11 years under the more recent statutory and Senate PAYGO rules. Congress cannot develop the revenue estimates simply by referring to the text of the legislation being scored. It must also take into account the behavior of taxpayers, economic conditions, and other factors that affect revenue collection.

Congress scores revenue and direct spending legislation by reference to baseline projections issued by CBO, sometimes in cooperation with OMB. The baseline is an extrapolation of future budget conditions, typically for each of the next five years, based on the assumption that current policies will continue in effect. The baseline projections incorporate assumptions about future inflation and workload changes mandated by law. These projections are made for the budget aggregates as well as for individual programs and accounts.

When Congress considers revenue or direct spending legislation, CBO estimates the amount of revenues or outlays that would ensue if the measure were enacted; in the case of most revenue legislation, CBO uses estimates prepared by the Joint Tax Committee. It then compares this amount with the baseline projection to score the legislation. Thus, the score measures budgetary impact as the difference between the amount projected under current policies and the amount estimated if the legislation were enacted. A score is reported for each of the years and often for the sum of the years as well.

Congress usually relies on the CBO score while it is considering legislation. The BEA gave OMB the authority to determine whether offsets or a sequester were required under the PAYGO rules. The more recent Statutory Pay-As-You-Go Act of 2010 provides that the budgetary effects of individual direct spending and revenue legislation are to be determined either by a reference in the legislation to a statement of budgetary effects submitted for printing in the *Congressional Record* by the chair of the House or Senate Budget Committee prior to passage, or by OMB if no appropriate reference in the legislation or statement exists. The OMB and CBO scores on legislation sometimes differ.

In addition to enforcing PAYGO, baseline projections and scoring are used in computing the amount of deficit reduction agreed to in budget summit negotiations between the President and Congress and enacted in reconciliation acts.

Budgeting for Direct and Guaranteed Loans

The Federal Credit Reform Act of 1990 made fundamental changes in the budgetary treatment of direct loans and guaranteed loans. The reform, which first became effective for FY1992, shifted the accounting basis for federally provided or guaranteed credit from the amount of cash flowing into or out of the Treasury to the estimated subsidy cost of the loans. Credit reform entails complex procedures for estimating these subsidy costs and new accounting mechanisms for recording various loan transactions. The changes have had only a modest impact on budget totals but a substantial impact on budgeting for particular loan programs.

The new system requires that budget authority and outlays be budgeted for the estimated subsidy cost of direct and guaranteed loans. This cost is defined in the 1990 act as "the estimated long- term cost to the Government of a direct loan or a loan guarantee, calculated on a net present value basis, excluding administrative costs."

Under the new system, Congress appropriates budget authority or provides indefinite authority equal to the subsidy cost. This budget authority is placed in a program account from which funds are disbursed to a financing account.

THE BUDGET CYCLE

Federal budgeting is a cyclical activity that begins with the formulation of the President's annual budget and concludes with the audit and review of expenditures. The process spreads over a multi-year period. The main stages are formulation of the President's budget, congressional budget actions, implementation of the budget, and audit and review. While the basic steps continue from year to year, particular procedures often vary in accord with the style of the President, the economic and political considerations under which the budget is prepared and implemented, and other factors.

The activities related to a single fiscal year usually stretch over a period of two-and-a-half calendar years (or longer). As the budget is being considered, federal agencies must deal with three different fiscal years at the same time: implementing the budget for the current fiscal year; seeking funds from Congress for the next fiscal year; and planning for the fiscal year after that.

THE PRESIDENTIAL BUDGET PROCESS

The President's budget, officially referred to as the *Budget of the United States Government*, is required by law to be submitted to Congress early in the legislative session, no later than the first Monday in February. The budget consists of estimates of spending, revenues, borrowing, and debt; policy and legislative recommendations; detailed estimates of the financial operations of federal agencies and programs; data on the actual and projected performance of the economy; and other information supporting the President's recommendations.

The President's budget is only a request to Congress; Congress is not required to adopt his recommendations. Nevertheless, the power to formulate and submit the budget is a vital tool in the President's direction of the executive branch and of national policy. The President's proposals often influence congressional revenue and spending decisions, though the extent of the influence varies from year to year and depends more on political and fiscal conditions than on the legal status of the budget.

The Constitution does not provide for a budget, nor does it require the President to make recommendations concerning the revenues and spending of the federal government. Until 1921, the federal government operated without a comprehensive presidential budget process. The Budget and Accounting Act of 1921, as amended, provides for a national budget system. Its basic requirement is that the President should prepare and submit a budget to Congress each year. The 1921 act established the Bureau of the Budget, now named the Office of Management and Budget (OMB), to assist the President in preparing and implementing the executive budget. Although it has been amended many times, this statute provides the legal basis for the presidential budget, prescribes much of its content, and defines the roles of the President and the agencies in the process.

Formulation and Content of the President's Budget

Preparation of the President's budget typically begins in the spring (or earlier) each year, at least nine months before the budget is submitted to Congress, about 17 months before the start of the fiscal year to which it pertains, and about 29 months before the close of that fiscal year. The early stages of budget preparation occur in federal agencies. When they begin work on the budget for a fiscal year, agencies already are implementing the budget for the fiscal year in progress and awaiting final appropriations actions and other legislative decisions for the fiscal year after that. The long lead times and the fact that appropriations have not yet been made for the next year mean that the budget is prepared with a great deal of uncertainty about economic conditions, presidential policies, and congressional actions.

As agencies formulate their budgets, they maintain continuing contact with the OMB examiners assigned to them. These contacts provide agencies with guidance in preparing their budgets and also enable them to alert OMB to any needs or problems that may loom ahead. Agency requests are submitted to OMB in late summer or early fall; these are reviewed by OMB staff in consultation with the President and his aides. The 1921 Budget and Accounting Act bars agencies from submitting their budget requests directly to Congress. Moreover, OMB regulations provide for confidentiality in all budget requests and recommendations prior to the transmittal of the

President's budget to Congress. However, it is quite common for internal budget documents to become public while the budget is still being formulated.

The format and content of the budget are partly determined by law, but the 1921 act authorizes the President to set forth the budget "in such form and detail" as he may determine. Over the years, there has been an increase in the types of information and explanatory material presented in the budget documents.

In most years, the budget is submitted as a multi-volume set consisting of a main document setting forth the President's message to Congress and an analysis and justification of his major proposals (the Budget) and supplementary documents providing account and program level details, historical information, and special budgetary analyses (the *Budget Appendix, Historical Tables*, and *Analytical Perspectives*), among other things.

Much of the budget is an estimate of requirements under existing law rather than a request for congressional action (more than half of the budget authority in the budget becomes available without congressional action). The President is required to submit a budget update (reflecting changed economic conditions, congressional actions, and other factors), referred to as the *Mid-Session Review*, by July 15 each year. The President may revise his recommendations any time during the year.

Executive Interaction with Congress

The President and his budget office have an important role once the budget is submitted to Congress. OMB officials and other presidential advisors appear before congressional committees to discuss overall policy and economic issues, but they generally leave formal discussions of specific programs to the affected agencies. Agencies thus bear the principal responsibility for defending the President's program recommendations at congressional hearings.

Agencies are supposed to justify the President's recommendations, not their own. OMB maintains an elaborate legislative clearance process to ensure that agency budget justifications, testimony, and other submissions are consistent with presidential policy. As the session unfolds, the President may formally signal his position on pending legislation through the issuance of a Statement of Administration Policy (SAP). These statements, which are maintained by OMB on its website, are sometimes used to convey a veto threat against legislation the President feels requires modifications to meet his approval.

Increasingly in recent years, the President and his chief budgetary aides have engaged in extensive negotiations with Congress over major budgetary legislation. These negotiations sometimes have occurred as formal budget "summits" and at other times as less visible, behind- the-scenes activities.

THE CONGRESSIONAL BUDGET PROCESS

The Congressional Budget and Impoundment Control Act of 1974 establishes the congressional budget process as the means by which Congress coordinates the various budget-related actions (such as the consideration of appropriations and revenue measures) taken by it during the course of the year. The process is centered around an annual concurrent resolution on the budget that sets aggregate budget policies and functional priorities for at least the next five fiscal years.

Because a concurrent resolution is not a law—it cannot be signed or vetoed by the President—the budget resolution does not have statutory effect; no money can be raised or spent pursuant to it. The main purpose of the budget resolution is to establish the framework within which Congress considers separate revenue, spending, and other budget-related legislation. Revenue and spending amounts set in the budget resolution establish the basis for the enforcement of congressional budget policies through points of order. The budget resolution also initiates the reconciliation process for conforming existing revenue and spending laws to congressional budget policies.

Formulation and Content of the Budget Resolution

The congressional budget process begins upon the presentation of the President's budget in January or February (see **Table 1**). The timetable set forth in the 1974 Congressional Budget Act calls for the final adoption of the budget resolution by April 15, well before the beginning of the new fiscal year on October 1. Although the House and Senate often pass the budget resolution separately before April 15, they often do not reach final agreement on it until after the deadline— sometimes months later. The 1974 act bars consideration of revenue, spending, and debt-limit measures for the upcoming fiscal year until the budget resolution for that year has been adopted, but certain exceptions are provided (such as the exception that allows the House to consider the regular appropriations bills after May 15, even if the budget resolution has not been adopted by then).

The 1974 Congressional Budget Act requires the budget resolution, for each fiscal year covered, to set forth budget aggregates and spending levels for each functional category of the budget. The aggregates included in the budget resolution are as follows:

- total revenues (and the amount by which the total is to be changed by legislative action);
- total new budget authority and outlays;
- the surplus or deficit; and
- the debt limit.

With regard to each of the functional categories, the budget resolution must indicate for each fiscal year the amounts of new budget authority and outlays, and they must add up to the corresponding spending or aggregates.

Table 1. Congressional Budget Process Timetable

Deadline	**Action to be completed**
First Monday in February	President submits budget to Congress.
February 15	CBO submits report on economic and budget outlook to Budget committees.
Six weeks after President's budget is submitted	Committees submit reports on views and estimates to respective Budget Committee.
April 1	Senate Budget Committee reports budget resolution.
April 15	Congress completes action on budget resolution.
June 10	House Appropriations Committee reports last regular appropriations bill.
June 30	House completes action on regular appropriations bills and any required reconciliation legislation.
July 15	President submits mid-session review of his budget to Congress.
October 1	Fiscal year begins.

Source: Compiled by the Congressional Research Service.

Aggregate amounts in the budget resolution do not reflect the revenues or spending of the Social Security trust funds, although these amounts are set forth separately in the budget resolution for purposes of Senate enforcement procedures.

The budget resolution does not allocate funds among specific programs or accounts, but the major program assumptions underlying the functional amounts are often discussed in the reports accompanying each resolution. Some recent reports have contained detailed information on the program levels assumed in the resolution. These assumptions are not binding on the affected committees. Finally, the 1974 act allows certain additional matters to be included in the budget resolution. The most important optional feature of a budget resolution is reconciliation directives (discussed below).

The House and Senate Budget Committees are responsible for marking up and reporting the budget resolution. In the course of developing the budget resolution, the Budget Committees hold hearings, receive "views and estimates" reports from other committees, and obtain information from CBO. These "views and estimates" reports of House and Senate committees provide the Budget Committees with information on the preferences and legislative plans of congressional committees regarding budgetary matters within their jurisdiction.

CBO assists the Budget Committees in developing the budget resolution by issuing, early each year, a report on the economic and budget outlook that includes baseline budget projections. The baseline projections presented in the report are supported by more detailed projections for accounts and programs; CBO usually revises the baseline projections one or more times before the Budget Committees mark up the budget resolution. In addition, CBO issues a report analyzing the President's budgetary proposals in light of CBO's own economic and technical assumptions. In past years, CBO also issued an annual report on spending and revenue options for reducing the deficit or maintaining the surplus.

The extent to which the Budget Committees (and the House and Senate) consider particular programs when they act on the budget resolution varies from year to year. Specific program decisions are supposed to be left to the Appropriations Committees and other committees of jurisdiction, but there is a strong likelihood that major issues will be discussed in markup, in the Budget Committees' reports, and during floor consideration of the budget resolution. Although any programmatic assumptions generated in this process are not binding on the committees of jurisdiction, they often influence the final outcome.

Floor consideration of the budget resolution is guided by House and Senate rules and practices. In the House, the Rules Committee usually reports a *special rule* (a simple House resolution), which, once approved, establishes the terms and conditions under which the budget resolution is considered. This special rule typically specifies which amendments may be considered and the sequence in which they are to be offered and voted on. It has been the practice in recent years to allow consideration of a few amendments (as substitutes for the entire resolution) that present broad policy choices. In the Senate, the amendment process is less structured, relying on agreements reached by the leadership through a broad consultative process. The amendments offered in the Senate may entail major policy choices or may be focused on a single issue.

Achievement of the policies set forth in the annual budget resolution depends on the legislative actions taken by Congress (and their approval or disapproval by the President), the performance of the economy, and technical considerations. Many of the factors that determine whether budgetary goals will be met are beyond the direct control of Congress. If economic conditions—growth, employment levels, inflation, and so forth—vary significantly from projected levels, so too will actual levels of revenue and spending. Similarly, actual levels may differ substantially if the technical factors upon which estimates are based, such as the rate at which agencies spend their discretionary funds or participants become eligible for entitlement programs, prove faulty.

Budget Resolution Enforcement

Congress's regular tools for enforcing the budget resolution each year are overall spending ceilings and revenue floors and committee allocations and subdivisions of spending. In addition, the Senate in some years has enforced discretionary spending limits in the budget resolution, which paralleled the adjustable limits established in statute and enforced by the sequestration process, and both chambers have imposed additional rules on direct spending and revenue legislation. Finally, the House and Senate in recent years have included procedural features in budget resolutions to limit the use of advance appropriations.

In order for the enforcement procedures to work, Congress must have access to complete and up- to-date budgetary information so that it can relate individual measures to overall budget policies and determine whether adoption of a particular measure would be consistent with those policies. Substantive and procedural points of order are designed to obtain congressional compliance with budget rules. A point of order may bar House or Senate consideration of legislation that violates the spending ceilings and revenue floors in the budget resolution, committee subdivisions of spending, or congressional budget procedures.

Budget Resolution Aggregates

In the early years after the 1974 Congressional Budget Act, the principal enforcement mechanism was the ceiling on total budget authority and outlays and the floor under total revenues set forth in the budget resolution. The limitations inherent in this mechanism soon became apparent. For example, the issue of controlling breaches of the spending ceilings usually did not arise until Congress acted on supplemental appropriations acts, when the fiscal year was well underway. The emergency nature of the legislation often made it difficult to uphold the ceilings.

Changes sometimes are made in budget resolutions by virtue of the operation of reserve funds. Generally, reserve funds allow increases to be made in various spending levels associated with the budget resolution for legislation meeting criteria specified in the budget resolution, as long as any increases spending from the legislation is offset (e.g., by revenue increases) so as to be deficit neutral.

Allocations of Spending to Committees

In view of the inadequacies in the early years of congressional budgeting of relying on enforcement of the budget totals, Congress changed the focus of enforcement in the 1980s to the committee allocations and subdivisions of spending made pursuant to Section 302 of the act. The key to enforcing budget policy is to relate the budgetary impact of individual pieces of legislation to the overall budget policy. Because Congress operates through its committee system, an essential step in linking particular measures to the budget is to allocate the spending amounts set forth in the budget resolution among House and Senate committees.

Section 302(a) provides for allocations to committees to be made in the statement of managers accompanying the conference report on the budget resolution. A Section 302(a) allocation is made to each committee which has jurisdiction over spending, both for the budget year and the full period covered by the budget resolution—at least five fiscal years.

The committee allocations do not take into account jurisdiction over discretionary authorizations funded in annual appropriations acts. The amounts of new budget authority and outlays allocated to committees in the House or Senate may not exceed the aggregate amounts of budget authority and outlays set forth in the budget resolution. Although these allocations are made by the Budget Committees, they are not the unilateral preferences of these committees. They are based on assumptions and understandings developed in the course of formulating the budget resolution.

After the allocations are made under Section 302(a), the House and Senate Appropriations Committees subdivide the amounts they receive among their 12 subcommittees, as required by Section 302(b). The subcommittees' Section 302(b) subdivisions may not exceed the total amount allocated to the committee. Each Appropriations Committee reports its subdivisions to its respective chamber; the appropriations bills may not be considered until such a report has been filed.

Scoring and Cost Estimates

As mentioned previously, scoring (also called scorekeeping) is the process of measuring the budgetary effects of pending and enacted legislation and assessing its impact on a budget plan— in this case, the budget resolution. In the congressional budget process, scoring serves several broad purposes. First, scoring informs members of Congress and the public about the budgetary consequences of their actions. When a budgetary measure is under consideration, scoring information lets members know whether adopting the amendment or passing the bill at hand would breach the budget. Further, scoring information enables members to judge what must be done in upcoming legislative action to achieve the year's budgetary goals. Finally, scoring is designed to assist Congress in enforcing its budget plans. In this regard, scorekeeping is used largely to determine whether points of order under the 1974 act may be sustained against legislation violating budget resolution levels.

The principal scorekeepers for Congress are the House and Senate Budget Committees, which provide the presiding officers of their respective chambers with the estimates needed to determine if legislation violates the aggregate levels in the budget resolution or the committee subdivisions of spending. The Budget Committees make summary scoring reports available to members on a frequent basis, usually geared to the pace of legislative activity. CBO assists Congress in these activities by preparing cost estimates of legislation, which are included in committee reports, and scoring reports for the Budget committees. The Joint Committee on Taxation supports Congress by preparing estimates of the budgetary impact of revenue legislation.

Points of Order

The 1974 Congressional Budget Act provides for both substantive and procedural points of order to block violations of budget resolution policies and congressional budget procedures. One element of substantive enforcement is based on Section 311 of the act, which bars Congress from considering legislation that would cause total revenues to fall below the level set in the budget resolution or total new budget authority or total outlays to exceed the budgeted level. The House and Senate both enforce the spending ceilings for the first fiscal year only; the revenue floor, however, is enforced for the first fiscal year and the full number of fiscal years covered by the budget resolution.

In the House (but not the Senate), Section 311 does not apply to spending legislation if the committee reporting the measure has stayed within its allocation of new discretionary budget authority. Accordingly, the House may take up any spending measure that is within the appropriate committee allocations, even if it would cause total spending to be exceeded. Neither chamber bars spending legislation that would cause functional allocations in the budget resolution to be exceeded.

Section 302(f) of the 1974 act bars the House and Senate from considering any spending measure that would cause the relevant committee's spending allocations to be exceeded; in the House, the point of order applies only to violations of allocations of new discretionary budget authority. Further, the point of order also applies to suballocations of spending made by the Appropriations Committees.

In addition to points of order to enforce compliance with the budget resolution and the allocations and subdivisions made pursuant to it, the 1974 act contains points of order to ensure compliance with its procedures. Perhaps the most important of these is Section 303, which bars consideration of any revenue, spending, entitlement, or debt-limit measure prior to adoption of the budget resolution. However, the rules of the House permit it to consider regular appropriations bills after May 15, even if the budget resolution has not yet been adopted.

When the House or Senate considers a revenue or a spending measure, the chairman of the respective Budget Committee sometimes makes a statement advising the chamber as to whether the measure violates any of these points of order. If no point of order is made, or if the point of order is waived, the House or Senate may consider a measure despite any violations of the 1974 act. The House often waives points of order by adopting a special rule. The Senate may waive points of order by unanimous consent or by motion under Section 904 of the act. The Senate requires a three-fifths vote of the membership to waive certain provisions of the act.

In several past years, the House and Senate failed to reach agreement on a budget resolution. On these occasions, one or both houses agreed to their own "deeming resolutions," which established the basis for enforcing points of order under the 1974 act in that house only.

THE SEQUESTRATION PROCESS

Sequestration was the principle means used to enforce statutory budget enforcement policies in place from 1985 through 2002, and it is the principle means used to enforce the PAYGO requirement under the Statutory Pay-As-You-Go Act of 2010 and the statutory limits on discretionary spending under the Budget Control Act of 2011 (BCA). In addition, sequestration is used to achieve a portion of the spending reductions required as a result of the failure to enact deficit reduction legislation tied to the Joint Committee on Deficit Reduction, as provided by the BCA.[2]

Sequestration involves the issuance of a presidential order that permanently cancels budgetary resources (except for revolving funds, special funds, trust funds, and certain offsetting collections) for the purpose of achieving a required amount of outlay savings to reduce the deficit. Once sequestration is triggered by an executive determination, spending reductions are made automatically; this process, therefore, is regarded by many as providing a strong incentive for Congress and the President to reach agreement on legislation that would avoid a sequester.

From its inception in 1985 until its revision by the Budget Enforcement Act (BEA) in 1990, the process was tied solely to the enforcement of fixed deficit targets. The BEA changed the sequestration process substantially. First, it effectively eliminated the deficit targets as a factor in budget enforcement. Second, the BEA established adjustable limits on discretionary spending funded in the annual appropriations process. Third, the BEA created pay-as-you-go procedures to require that increases in direct spending (i.e., spending controlled outside of the annual appropriations process) or decreases in revenues due to legislative action were offset so that there was effectively no net increase in the deficit or reduction of the surplus.

The BEA established adjustable limits on discretionary spending for FY1991-FY1995. These limits were extended through FY1998 in 1993. The Budget Enforcement Act (BEA) of 1997 revised the limits for FY1998 and provided new limits through FY2002. The limits were established for the following categories of discretionary spending: defense and nondefense, for FY1998-FY1999; discretionary (a single, general purpose category), for FY2000-FY2002; and violent crime reduction, for FY1998-FY2000. In 1998, as part of the Transportation Equity Act for the 21st Century, separate categories were added for highway and mass transit spending. Finally, a spending conservation category was added in 2000. The limits expired at the end of FY2002. As noted above, the Budget Control Act of 2011 revived the statutory limits on discretionary spending by establishing them for each year through FY2021.

The original discretionary spending limits had to be adjusted periodically by the President for various factors, including (among others), changes in concepts and definitions, a special outlay allowance (to accommodate estimating differences between OMB and CBO), and the enactment of legislation providing emergency funding and funding for the International Monetary Fund, international arrearages, an earned income tax credit compliance initiative, and other specially designated purposes. The more recent limits, under the BCA, may be adjusted for spending designated for emergencies, Overseas Contingency Operations, and disaster relief, among other specified purposes.

Under the pay-as-you-go (PAYGO) process created by the BEA, legislation increasing direct spending or decreasing revenues for a fiscal year had to be offset so that the balance on the PAYGO scorecard for that year did not fall below zero. The PAYGO process did not require any offsetting action when the spending increase or revenue decrease was due to the operation of existing law, such as an increase in the number of persons participating in the Medicare program. Direct spending consists largely of spending for entitlement programs. Most direct spending and revenue programs are established under permanent law, so there is not necessarily any need for recurring legislative action on them (and the PAYGO process did not require such action).

The PAYGO process did not preclude Congress from enacting legislation to increase direct spending; it only required that the increase be offset by reductions in other direct spending programs (which could include increases in offsetting receipts), by increases in revenues, or by a combination of the two in order to avoid a sequester. If a sequester under this process was required, it would have had to offset the amount of any net deficit increase (or surplus reduction) for the fiscal year caused by the enactment of legislation in the current and prior sessions of Congress, and would have been applied to nonexempt direct spending programs.

Spending for Social Security benefits and federal deposit insurance commitments, as well as emergency direct spending and revenue legislation (so designated by both the President and by Congress), was exempted completely from the PAYGO sequestration process. All remaining direct spending programs were covered by the PAYGO process to the extent that legislation affecting their spending levels was counted in determining whether a net increase or decrease in the deficit has occurred for a fiscal year. If a PAYGO sequester had occurred, however, many direct spending programs would have been exempt from reduction.

In 1997, coverage of the PAYGO requirement was extended to legislation enacted through FY2002; however, the PAYGO process was slated to remain in effect through FY2006 to deal with the outyear effects of such measures. Consequently, a PAYGO sequester could have occurred in FY2003-FY2006 based on legislation enacted before the end of FY2002. At the end of the 107th Congress, legislation was enacted setting all of the remaining PAYGO balances to zero, effectively terminating the PAYGO requirement under the BEA.

The multiple sequestration procedures established by the BEA remained automatic, to be triggered by a report from the OMB director. For sequestration purposes generally, there was only one triggering report issued each year (just after the end of the congressional session), but preliminary and update sequestration reports were issued earlier in the session. Additionally, OMB reports triggering a sequester for discretionary spending could be issued during the following session if legislative developments so warranted (i.e., the enactment of supplemental appropriations). The CBO director was required to provide advisory sequestration reports, shortly before the OMB director's reports were due.

Sequestration procedures could be suspended in the event a declaration of war was enacted or if Congress enacted a special joint resolution triggered by the issuance of a CBO report indicating "low growth" in the economy. Also, there were several special procedures under the act by which the final sequestration order for a fiscal year could be modified or the implementation of the order affected.

As noted above, sequestration has been revived to enforce more recent statutory budget enforcement rules. First, the Statutory Pay-As-You-Go Act of

2010, enacted on February 12, 2010, restored the sequestration process to enforce the new PAYGO requirement for direct spending and revenue legislation. Generally, the new statutory PAYGO process provides that if the net effect of direct spending and revenue legislation enacted during a year increases the deficit, budgetary resources in certain direct spending programs are cut in order to eliminate the increase in the deficit. Specifically, the average budgetary effects (i.e., any increase or decrease in the deficit) over five- and 10-year periods[3] of each direct spending and revenue act are placed on five- and 10-year scorecards, respectively. Like the PAYGO process under the BEA, the sequestration process is triggered by a report from the OMB director issued 14 days after Congress adjourns at the end of a session. If either scorecard shows a positive balance (referred to as a debit) for the budget year, the President is required to issue a sequestration order cancelling budgetary resources in non-exempt direct spending programs sufficient to eliminate the balance (the larger balance if both scorecards show a positive balance).[4]

Second, the Budget Control Act of 2011 restored the sequestration process, including the reports and triggering mechanisms under the earlier BEA, to enforce the recently established statutory limits on discretionary spending for each fiscal year through FY2021. In addition, the BCA uses sequestration to achieve additional deficit reduction. Specifically, the BCA created a Joint Select Committee on Deficit Reduction, composed of an equal number of Senators and Members of the House, and instructed it to develop a proposal that would reduce the deficit by at least $1.5 trillion over the FY2012-FY2021 period. In the event that this Joint Committee was not successful, the BCA established the automatic process to reduce spending (a fallback mechanism to automatically reduce spending), beginning in 2013. If legislation developed by the Joint Committee did not reduce the deficit by at least $1.2 trillion through FY2021 and was not enacted by January 15, 2012, this automatic process would be triggered. The process presumably was intended to encourage agreement on such deficit reduction, either by enacting the Joint Committee proposal or possibly by enacting other legislation (through existing congressional procedures) prior to the beginning of 2013, when the automatic process would begin to make reductions. Given that the Joint Committee was not successful, this automatic process has been triggered. Therefore, at the time of this writing, spending reductions are scheduled to be made on January 2, 2013, with a sequester of $109 billion in budgetary resources equally divided between defense and nondefense spending, unless Congress and the President agree by statute to repeal or modify the automatic process. Additional spending reductions are also scheduled to be achieved in direct spending in each year through FY2021.

SPENDING LEGISLATION

The spending policies of the budget resolution generally are implemented through two different types of spending legislation. Policies involving discretionary spending are implemented in the context of annual appropriations acts, whereas policies affecting direct or mandatory spending (which, for the most part, involves entitlement programs) are carried out in substantive legislation.

All discretionary spending is under the jurisdiction of the House and Senate Appropriations Committees. Direct spending is under the jurisdiction of the various legislative committees of the House and Senate; the House Ways and Means Committee and the Senate Finance Committee have the largest shares of direct spending jurisdiction. (Some entitlement programs, such as Medicaid, are funded in annual appropriations acts, but such spending is not considered to be discretionary.) The enforcement procedures under the congressional budget process, mentioned above, apply equally to discretionary and direct spending.

Authorizing Measures

The rules of the House and (to a lesser extent) the Senate require that agencies and programs be authorized in law before an appropriation is made for them. An authorizing act is a law that (1) establishes a program or agency and the terms and conditions under which it operates; and (2) authorizes the enactment of appropriations for that program or agency. Authorizing legislation may originate in either the House or the Senate and may be considered any time during the year. Many agencies and programs have temporary authorizations that have to be renewed annually or every few years.

Action on appropriations measures sometimes is delayed by the failure of Congress to enact necessary authorizing legislation. The House and Senate often waive or disregard their rules against unauthorized appropriations for ongoing programs that have not yet been reauthorized.

The budgetary impact of authorizing legislation depends on whether it contains only discretionary authorizations (for which funding is provided in annual appropriations acts) or direct spending, which itself enables an agency to enter into obligations.

The Annual Appropriations Process

An appropriations act is a law passed by Congress that provides federal agencies legal authority to incur obligations and the Treasury Department authority to make payments for designated purposes. The power of appropriation derives from the Constitution, which in Article I, Section 9, provides that "[n]o money shall be drawn from the Treasury but in consequence of appropriations made by law." The power to appropriate is exclusively a legislative power; it functions as a limitation on the executive branch. An agency may not spend more than the amount appropriated to it, and it may use available funds only for the purposes and according to the conditions provided by Congress.

The Constitution does not require annual appropriations, but since the First Congress the practice has been to make appropriations for a single fiscal year. Appropriations must be used (obligated) in the fiscal year for which they are provided, unless the law provides that they shall be available for a longer period of time. All provisions in an appropriations act, such as limitations on the use of funds, expire at the end of the fiscal year, unless the language of the act extends their period of effectiveness.

The President requests annual appropriations in his budget submitted each year. In support of the President's appropriations requests, agencies submit justification materials to the House and Senate Appropriations Committees. These materials provide considerably more detail than is contained in the President's budget and are used in support of agency testimony during Appropriations subcommittee hearings on the President's budget.

Congress passes three main types of appropriations measures. *Regular appropriations* acts provide budget authority to agencies for the next fiscal year. *Supplemental appropriations* acts provide additional budget authority during the current fiscal year when the regular appropriation is insufficient or to finance activities not provided for in the regular appropriation. *Continuing appropriations* acts provide stop-gap (or full-year) funding for agencies that have not received a regular appropriation.

In a typical session, Congress acts on 12 regular appropriations bills and at least two supplemental appropriations measures. Because of recurring delays in the appropriations process, Congress also typically passes one or more continuing appropriations each year. The scope and duration of these measures depend on the status of the regular appropriations bills and the degree of budgetary conflict between the President and Congress. In recent years, Congress has merged two or more of the regular appropriations acts for a fiscal year into a single, omnibus appropriations act.

By precedent, appropriations originate in the House of Representatives. In the House, appropriations measures are originated by the Appropriations Committee (when it marks up or reports the measure) rather than being introduced by a member beforehand. Before the full Committee acts on the bill, it is considered in the relevant Appropriations subcommittee (the House and Senate Appropriations Committees have 12 parallel subcommittees). The House subcommittees typically hold extensive hearings on appropriations requests shortly after the President's budget is submitted. In marking up their appropriations bills, the various subcommittees are guided by the discretionary spending limits and the allocations made to them under Section 302 of the 1974 Congressional Budget Act.

The Senate usually considers appropriations measures after they have been passed by the House. When House action on appropriations bills is delayed, however, the Senate sometimes expedites its actions by considering a Senate-numbered bill up to the stage of final passage. Upon receipt of the House-passed bill in the Senate, it is amended with the text that the Senate already has agreed to (as a single amendment) and then passed by the Senate. Hearings in the Senate Appropriations subcommittees generally are not as extensive as those held by counterpart subcommittees in the House.

The basic unit of an appropriation is an account. A single unnumbered paragraph in an appropriations act comprises one account and all provisions of that paragraph pertain to that account and to no other, unless the text expressly gives them broader scope. Any provision limiting the use of funds enacted in that paragraph is a restriction on that account alone.

Over the years, appropriations have been consolidated into a relatively small number of accounts. It is typical for a federal agency to have a single account for all its expenses of operation and additional accounts for other purposes such as construction. Accordingly, most appropriation accounts encompass a number of activities or projects. The appropriation sometimes earmarks specific amounts to particular activities within the account, but the more common practice is to provide detailed information on the amounts intended for each activity in other sources (principally, the committee reports accompanying the measures).

In addition to the substantive limitations (and other provisions) associated with each account, each appropriations act has "general provisions" that apply to all of the accounts in a title or in the whole act. These general provisions appear as numbered sections, usually at the end of the title or the act.

The standard appropriation is for a single fiscal year—the funds have to be obligated during the fiscal year for which they are provided; they lapse if not obligated by the end of that year. An appropriation that does not mention the period during which the funds are to be available is a one- year appropriation. Congress also makes no-year appropriations by specifying that the funds shall remain available until expended. No-year funds are carried over to future years, even if they have not been obligated. Congress sometimes makes multiyear appropriations, which provide for funds to be available for two or more fiscal years.

Appropriations measures also contain other types of provisions that serve specialized purposes. These include provisions that liquidate (pay off) obligations made pursuant to certain contract authority; reappropriate funds provided in previous years; transfer funds from one account to another; rescind funds (or release deferred funds); or set ceilings on the amount of obligations that can be made under permanent appropriations, on the amount of direct or guaranteed loans that can be made, or on the amount of administrative expenses that can be incurred during the fiscal year. In addition to providing funds, appropriations acts often contain substantive limitations on government agencies. Detailed information on how funds are to be spent, along with other directives or guidance, is provided in the reports accompanying the various appropriations measures. Agencies ordinarily abide by report language in spending the funds appropriated by Congress.

The appropriations reports do not comment on every item of expenditure. Report language is most likely when the Appropriations Committee prefers to spend more or less on a particular item than the President has requested or when the committee wants to earmark funds for a particular project or activity. When a particular item is mentioned by the committee, there is a strong expectation that the agency will adhere to the instructions.

REVENUE LEGISLATION

Article I, Section 8 of the Constitution gives Congress the power to levy "taxes, duties, imposts, and excises." Section 7 of this article requires that all revenue measures originate in the House of Representatives.

In the House, revenue legislation is under the jurisdiction of the Ways and Means Committee; in the Senate, jurisdiction is held by the Finance Committee. While House rules bar other committees from reporting revenue legislation, sometimes another committee will report legislation levying user fees on a class that benefits from a particular service or program or that is being regulated by a federal agency. In many of these cases, the user fee legislation is referred subsequently to the Ways and Means Committee.

Most revenues derive from existing provisions of the tax code or Social Security law, which continue in effect from year to year unless changed by Congress. This tax structure can be expected to produce increasing amounts of revenue in future years as the economy expands and incomes rise. Nevertheless, Congress usually makes some changes in the tax laws each year, either to raise or lower revenues or to redistribute the tax burden.

Congress typically acts on revenue legislation pursuant to proposals in the President's budget. An early step in congressional work on revenue legislation is publication by CBO of its own estimates (developed in consultation with the Joint Tax Committee) of the revenue impact of the President's budget proposals. The congressional estimates often differ significantly from those presented in the President's budget.

The revenue totals in the budget resolution establish the framework for subsequent action on revenue measures. The budget resolution contains only revenue totals and total recommended changes; it does not allocate these totals among revenue sources (although it does set out Medicare receipts separately), nor does it specify which provisions of the tax code are to be changed.

The House and Senate often consider major revenue measures, such as the Tax Reform Act of 1986, under their regular legislative procedures. However, as has been the case with direct spending programs, many of the most significant changes in revenue policy in recent years have been made in the context of the reconciliation process. Although revenue changes are usually incorporated into omnibus budget reconciliation measures, along with spending changes (and sometimes debt-limit increases), revenue reconciliation legislation may be considered on a separate legislative track (e.g., the Tax Equity and Fiscal Responsibility Act of 1982).

When the reconciliation process is used to advance revenue reductions (or spending increases) that would lead to a deficit, or would enlarge an existing deficit, Section 313 of the 1974 Congressional Budget Act (referred to as the Senate's "Byrd rule") limits the legislative changes to the period covered by the reconciliation directives. Accordingly, some recent tax cuts have been subject to sunset dates.

In enacting revenue legislation, Congress often establishes or alters tax expenditures. The term "tax expenditures" is defined in the 1974 Congressional Budget Act to include revenue losses due to deductions, exemptions, credits, and other exceptions to the basic tax structure. Tax expenditures are a means by which the federal government pursues public policy objectives and can be regarded as alternatives to other policy instruments such as grants or loans. The Joint Tax Committee estimates the revenue effects of legislation changing tax expenditures, and it also publishes five-year projections of these provisions as an annual committee print.

DEBT-LIMIT LEGISLATION

When the revenues collected by the federal government are not sufficient to cover its expenditures, it must finance the shortfall through borrowing. Federal borrowing is subject to a public debt limit established by statute. When the federal government operates with a budget deficit, the public debt limit must be increased periodically. The frequency of congressional action to raise the debt limit has ranged in the past from several times in one year to once in several years. When the federal government incurred large and growing surpluses in recent years, Congress did not have to increase the debt limit, but the enactment of increases in the debt limit has again become necessary with the recurrence of deficits.

Legislation to raise the public debt limit falls under the jurisdiction of the House Ways and Means Committee and the Senate Finance Committee. Although consideration of such measures in the House usually is constrained through the use of special rules, Senate action sometimes is far- ranging with regard to the issues covered. In the past, the Senate has added many non-germane provisions to debt-limit measures, such as the 1985 Balanced Budget Act.

In 1979, the House amended its rules to provide for the automatic engrossment of a measure increasing the debt limit upon final adoption of the conference report on the budget resolution. The rule, House Rule XLIX (commonly referred to as the Gephardt rule), was intended to facilitate quick action on debt increases. However, the Senate had no comparable rule. For years, the House and Senate could enact debt-limit legislation originating under the Gephardt rule or arising under conventional legislative procedures. During the past decade, Congress has enacted debt-limit increases as part of omnibus budget reconciliation measures, continuing appropriations acts, and other legislation. The House recodified the Gephardt rule as House Rule XXIII at the beginning of the 106th Congress, repealed it at the beginning of the 107th Congress, and reinstated it, as new Rule XXVII, at the beginning of the 108th Congress. At the beginning of the 112th Congress, the House once again repealed the rule, thereby requiring the House to vote directly on any legislation that changes the statutory limit on the public debt.

RECONCILIATION LEGISLATION

Beginning in 1980, Congress has used reconciliation legislation to implement many of its most significant budget policies. Section 310 of the 1974 Congressional Budget Act sets forth a special procedure for the development and consideration of reconciliation legislation. Reconciliation legislation is used by Congress to bring existing revenue and spending law into conformity with the policies in the budget resolution. Reconciliation is an optional process, but Congress has used it more years than not; during the period covering 1980 through 2010, 20 reconciliation measures were enacted into law and three were vetoed.

The reconciliation process has two stages—the adoption of reconciliation instructions in the budget resolution and the enactment of reconciliation legislation that implements changes in revenue or spending laws. Although reconciliation has been used since 1980, specific procedures tend to vary from year to year.

Reconciliation is used to change the amount of revenues, budget authority, or outlays generated by existing law. In a few instances, reconciliation has been used to adjust the public debt limit. On the spending side, the process focuses on entitlement laws; it may not be used, however, to impel changes in Social Security law. Reconciliation sometimes has been applied to discretionary authorizations (which are funded in annual appropriations acts), but this is not the usual practice.

Reconciliation was used in the 1980s and into the 1990s as a deficit-reduction tool. Beginning in the latter part of the 1990s, some reconciliation measures were used principally to reduce revenues, thereby increasing the deficit. At the beginning of the 110th Congress, both chambers adopted rules requiring that reconciliation be used solely for deficit reduction.

Reconciliation Directives

Reconciliation begins with a directive in a budget resolution instructing designated committees to report legislation changing existing law or pending legislation. These instructions have three components: (1) they name the committee (or committees) that are directed to report legislation; (2) they specify the amounts by which existing laws are to be changed (but do not identify how these changes are to be made, which laws are to be altered, or the programs to be affected); and (3) they usually set a deadline by which the designated committees are to recommend the changes in law. The instructions typically cover the same fiscal years covered by the budget resolution. Sometimes, budget resolutions have provided for more than one reconciliation measure to be considered during a session.

The dollar amounts are computed with reference to the CBO baseline. Thus, a change represents the amount by which revenues or spending would decrease or increase from baseline levels as a result of changes made in existing law. This computation is itself based on assumptions about the future level of revenues or spending under current law (or policy) and about the dollar changes that would ensue from new legislation. Hence, the savings associated with the reconciliation process are assumed savings. The actual changes in revenues or spending may differ from those estimated when the reconciliation instructions are formulated.

Although the instructions do not mention the programs to be changed, they are based on assumptions as to the savings or deficit reduction (or, in some cases, increases) that would result from particular changes in revenue provisions or spending programs. These program assumptions are sometimes printed in the reports on the budget resolution. Even when the assumptions are not published, committees and members usually have a good idea of the specific program changes contemplated by the reconciliation instructions.

A committee has discretion to decide on the legislative changes to be recommended. It is not bound by the program changes recommended or assumed by the Budget Committees in the reports accompanying the budget resolution. Further, a committee has to recommend legislation estimated to produce dollar changes for each category delineated in the instructions to it.

When a budget resolution containing a reconciliation instruction has been approved by Congress, the instruction has the status of an order by the House and Senate to designated committees to recommend legislation, usually by a date certain. It is expected that committees will carry out the instructions of their parent chamber, but the 1974 Congressional Budget Act does not provide any sanctions against committees that fail to do so.

Development and Consideration of Reconciliation Measures

When more than one committee in the House and Senate is subject to reconciliation directives, the proposed legislative changes usually are consolidated by the Budget Committees into an omnibus bill. The 1974 Congressional Budget Act does not permit the Budget Committees to revise substantively the legislation recommended by the committees of jurisdiction. This restriction pertains even when the Budget Committees estimate that the proposed legislation will fall short of the dollar changes called for in the instructions. Sometimes, the Budget Committees, working with the leadership, develop alternatives to the committee recommendations, to be offered as floor amendments, so as to achieve greater compliance with the reconciliation directives.

The 1974 act requires that amendments offered to reconciliation legislation in either the House or the Senate be deficit neutral. To meet this requirement, an amendment reducing revenues or increasing spending must offset these deficit increases by equivalent revenue increases or spending cuts.

During the first several years' experience with reconciliation, the legislation contained many provisions that were extraneous to the purpose of reducing the deficit. The reconciliation submissions of committees included such things as provisions that had no budgetary effect, that increased spending or reduced revenues, or that violated another committee's jurisdiction.

In 1985, the Senate adopted a rule (commonly referred to as the Byrd rule) on a temporary basis as a means of curbing these practices. The Byrd rule has been extended and modified several times over the years. In 1990, the Byrd rule was incorporated into the 1974 Congressional Budget Act as Section 313 and made permanent.

Although the House has no rule comparable to the Senate's Byrd rule, it may use other devices to control the inclusion of extraneous matter in reconciliation legislation. In particular, the House may use special rules to make in order amendments that strike such matter.

House and Senate Earmark Disclosure Rules

In 2007, both the House and Senate adopted rules intended to bring more transparency to the process surrounding earmarks. Although the definitions vary, an earmark generally is considered to be an allocation of resources to specifically targeted beneficiaries, either through discretionary or direct spending, limited tax benefits, or limited tariff benefits.[5]

Concern about earmarking practices arose over such provisions being inserted into legislation or accompanying reports without any identification of the sponsor, and the belief that many earmarks were not subject to proper scrutiny and diverted resources to lesser-priority items or items without sufficient justification, thereby contributing to wasteful spending or revenue loss.

In response to this concern, earmark rules were adopted that vary by chamber, but include three main features. The first feature is a requirement that members requesting a congressional earmark provide a written statement to the chair and ranking minority member of the committee of jurisdiction that includes the member's name, the name and address of the intended earmark recipient, the purpose of the earmark, and a certification that the member or member's spouse has no financial interest in such an earmark. (The Senate rule applies not only to the spouse but the entire immediate family.)

The second feature is a general requirement that committees provide a list of all earmarks included in reported legislation. The third feature is a point of order against legislation that is not accompanied by a list of included earmarks. These vary by chamber.

House of Representatives

House Rule XXI, clause 9, generally requires that certain types of measures be accompanied by a list of earmarks or a statement that the measure contains no earmarks.[6] If the list of earmarks or the statement that no earmark exists in the measure is absent, a point of order may lie against the measure's floor consideration. The point of order applies to the absence of such a list or statement, and does not speak to the completeness or the accuracy of such document.

House earmark disclosure rules apply to any congressional earmark included in either the text of the measure or the committee report accompanying the measure, as well as the conference report and joint explanatory statement. The disclosure requirements apply to items in authorizing, appropriations, and revenue legislation. Furthermore, they apply not only to measures reported by committees, but also to unreported measures, "manager's amendments," Senate measures, and conference reports.

These earmark disclosure requirements, however, do not apply to all legislation at all times. Not subject to the rule are floor amendments (except a "manager's amendment"), amendments between the Houses, or amendments considered as adopted under a self-executing special rule, including a committee amendment in the nature of a substitute made in order as original text. The earmark rule, as with most House rules, is not self enforcing and relies instead on a member raising a point of order if the rule is violated. When a measure is considered under suspension of the rules, House rules are laid aside and earmark disclosure rules are, therefore, waived. It is not in order to consider a special rule that waives earmark requirements under the House rule.

The Senate

Senate Rule XLIV creates a point of order against a motion to proceed to consider a measure or a vote on adoption of a conference report, unless the chair of the committee or the Majority Leader (or designee) certifies that a complete list of earmarks and the name of each Senator requesting each earmark is available on a publicly accessible congressional website in a searchable form at least 48 hours before the vote. If a Senator proposes a floor amendment containing an earmark, those items must be printed in the *Congressional Record* as soon as "practicable."[7] If the earmark certification requirements have not been met, a point of order may lie against consideration of the measure or a vote on the conference report. The point of order applies only to the absence of such certification, and does not speak to its accuracy.

Senate earmark disclosure rules apply to any congressional earmark included in either the text of the bill or a committee report accompanying the bill, as well as a conference report and joint explanatory statement. The disclosure requirements apply to items in authorizing, appropriations, and revenue legislation. Furthermore, they apply not only to measures reported by committees, but also to unreported measures, amendments, House bills, and conference reports.

The earmark rule may be waived either by unanimous consent or by motion, which requires the affirmative vote of three-fifths of all Senators (60, if there are no vacancies).[8] The earmark rule, as with most Senate rules, is not self enforcing and relies instead on a Senator raising a point of order if the rule is violated.

While not embodied in either chamber's rules, an earmark "ban" or "moratorium" is currently in effect in both the House and Senate, enforced by committee and chamber leadership.[9]

IMPOUNDMENT AND LINE-ITEM VETO

Impoundment

Although an appropriation limits the amounts that can be spent, it also establishes the expectation that the available funds will be used to carry out authorized activities. Therefore, when an agency fails to use all or part of an appropriation, it deviates from the intentions of Congress. The Impoundment Control Act of 1974 prescribes rules and procedures for instances in which available funds are impounded.

An impoundment is an action or inaction by the President or a federal agency that delays or withholds the obligation or expenditure of budget authority provided in law. The 1974 Impoundment Control Act divides impoundments into two categories and establishes distinct procedures for each. A *deferral* delays the use of funds; a *rescission* is a presidential request that Congress rescind (cancel) an appropriation or other form of budget authority. Deferral and rescission are exclusive and comprehensive categories; an impoundment is either a rescission or a deferral—it cannot be both or something else.

Although impoundments are defined broadly by the 1974 act, in practice they are limited to major actions that affect the level or rate of expenditure. As a general practice, only deliberate curtailments of expenditure are reported as impoundments; actions having other purposes that incidently affect the rate of spending are not recorded as impoundments. For example, if an agency were to delay the award of a contract because of a dispute with a vendor, the delay would not be an impoundment; if the delay were for the purpose of reducing an expenditure, it would be an impoundment. The line between routine administrative actions and impoundments is not clear and controversy occasionally arises as to whether a particular action constitutes an impoundment.

Rescissions

To propose a rescission, the President must submit a message to Congress specifying the amount to be rescinded, the accounts and programs involved, the estimated fiscal and program effects, and the reasons for the rescission. Multiple rescissions can be grouped in a single message. After the message has been submitted to it, Congress has 45 days of "continuous session" (usually a larger number of calendar days) during which it can pass a rescission bill. Congress may rescind all, part, or none of the amount proposed by the President.

If Congress does not approve a rescission in legislation by the expiration of this period, the President must make the funds available for obligation and expenditure. If the President fails to release funds at the expiration of the 45-day period for proposed rescissions, the comptroller general may bring suit to compel their release. This has been a rare occurrence, however.

Deferrals

To defer funds, the President submits a message to Congress setting forth the amount, the affected account and program, the reasons for the deferral, the estimated fiscal and program effects, and the period of time during which the funds are to be deferred. The President may not propose a deferral for a period of time beyond the end of the fiscal year, nor may he propose a deferral that would cause the funds to lapse or otherwise prevent an agency from spending appropriated funds prudently. In accounts where unobligated funds remain available beyond the fiscal year, the President may defer the funds again in the next fiscal year.

At present, the President may defer only for the reasons set forth in the Antideficiency Act, including to provide for contingencies, to achieve savings made possible by or through changes in requirements or greater efficiency of operations, and as specifically provided by law. He may not defer funds for policy reasons (e.g., to curtail overall federal spending or because he is opposed to a particular program).

The comptroller general reviews all proposed rescissions and deferrals and advises Congress of their legality and possible budgetary and program effects. The comptroller general also notifies Congress of any rescission or deferral not reported by the President and may reclassify an improperly classified impoundment. In all cases, a notification to Congress by the comptroller general has the same legal effect as an impoundment message of the President.

The 1974 Impoundment Control Act provides for special types of legislation—rescission bills and deferral resolutions—for Congress to use in exercising its impoundment control powers. However, pursuant to court decisions that held the legislative veto to be unconstitutional, Congress may not use deferral resolutions to disapprove a deferral. Further, Congress has been reluctant to use rescission bills regularly. Congress, instead, usually acts on impoundment matters within the framework of the annual appropriations measures.

Line-Item Veto

During the 104th Congress, the Line Item Veto Act (P.L. 104-130) was enacted as an amendment to the 1974 Impoundment Control Act. The Supreme Court ruled the Line Item Veto Act unconstitutional in June 1998.

The authority granted to the President under the Line Item Veto Act differed markedly from the veto authority available to most chief executives at the state level. First, the President could not veto individual parts of legislation submitted for his approval. Under normal constitutional procedures, the President must approve or veto any measure in its entirety. His authority to use the line-item veto came into play only after a measure had been signed into law. Second, this authority applied not only to annual appropriations, but extended to new entitlement spending and targeted tax benefits as well. The line-item veto authority was intended to be in effect for eight years, from the beginning of 1997 through the end of 2004.

The Line Item Veto Act reversed the presumption underlying the process for the consideration of rescissions under the 1974 Impoundment Control Act. Under the Line Item Veto Act, presidential proposals would take effect unless overturned by legislative action. The act authorized the President to identify at enactment individual items in legislation that he proposed not go into effect. The identification was based not just upon the statutory language, but on the entire legislative history and documentation. The President had to notify Congress promptly of his proposals and provide supporting information. Congress had to respond within a limited period of time by enacting a law if it wanted to disapprove the President's proposals; otherwise, they would take effect permanently.

President Clinton exercised the line-item veto authority several times during the 1997 session before the act was declared unconstitutional.

End Notes

[1] For more detailed information on the statutory PAYGO requirement, see CRS Report R41157, *The Statutory Pay-As-You-Go Act of 2010: Summary and Legislative History*, by Bill Heniff Jr.

[2] For further information on the BCA, see CRS Report R41965, *The Budget Control Act of 2011*, by Bill Heniff Jr., Elizabeth Rybicki, and Shannon M. Mahan.

[3] The five-year period covers the budget year and four fiscal years thereafter, and the 10-year period covers the budget year and nine fiscal years thereafter. The statutory rule also requires that any budgetary effects for the current year must be added to the budgetary effects for the budget year.

[4] Most direct spending programs and activities, including Social Security benefits, veterans' programs, retirement and disability benefits, and low-income programs, among others, are exempt from any sequestration. In addition, the amount of any sequestration is limited to 4% for Medicare and 2% for certain health and medical care activities.

[5] For more information on House and Senate earmark rules, see CRS Report RL34462, *House and Senate Procedural Rules Concerning Earmark Disclosure*, by Sandy Streeter.

[6] Depending upon the type of measure, the list or statement is to be included either in the measure's accompanying report, or printed in the *Congressional Record*.

[7] The rule does not apply to all earmarks in floor amendments, only those "not included in the bill or joint resolution as placed on the calendar or as reported by any committee, in a committee report on such a bill or joint resolution, or a committee report of the Senate on a companion measure," as stated in Rule XLIV, paragraph 4(a).

[8] These points of order may also be waived if the Majority and Minority Leaders jointly agree that "such a waiver is necessary as a result of a significant disruption to Senate facilities or to the availability of the Internet." Senate Rule XLIV, paragraph 12.

[9] The House Republican Conference Rules include a standing order, adopted December 8, 2010, stating that "It is the policy of the House Republican Conference that no Member shall request a congressional earmark, limited tax benefit, or limited tariff benefit, as such terms have been described in the Rules of the House," available at http://www.gop.gov/ about/rules?standing-orders-for-the-112th. In the Senate, the chair of the Committee on Appropriations announced in a press release on February 1, 2011, and again on February 2, 2012, that an earmark moratorium would be enforced on all FY2011, FY2012, and FY2013 appropriations bills, available at http://www.appropriations.senate.gov/news.cfm? method= news.view&id=188dc791-4b0d-459e-b8d9-4ede5ca299e7 and http://www.appropriations. senate.gov/news.cfm?method=news.view&id=3883059e-7a0c-496e-8d51-440aa7c2d57c.

In: Biennial Budgeting
Editor: Carolyn Douglas

ISBN: 978-1-63482-673-0

Chapter 4

ADOPTING A LONG-TERM BUDGET FOCUS: CHALLENGES AND PROPOSALS*

Megan Suzanne Lynch, Marc Labonte and Mindy R. Levit

SUMMARY

One criticism of the current budget process is that it does not encourage or require the consideration of long-term budgetary concerns. In this context, a long-term concern is one that affects the budget beyond the traditional five- or 10-year budget window as currently used in the congressional budget resolution and the President's budget.

Some components of the budget process already deal with long-term budget issues. This means that data already exist, in publicly available formats, to assist in evaluating the country's longterm fiscal health. In some instances, data evaluating the long-term outlook of certain programs are currently available, including on those programs that are generally thought of as the most challenging to deal with going forward. Long-term components of the budget process can be separated into two general categories and are currently used for two distinct purposes: long-term budgetary data used for informational purposes and rules affecting long-term outcomes that are used for enforcement purposes.

---

* This is an edited, reformatted and augmented version of a Congressional Research Service publication R41516, prepared for Members and Committees of Congress, dated January 13, 2011.

Proponents of more formal long-term budgeting have expressed concerns that the current process allows difficult long-term decisions to be avoided, hides the long-term effects of certain budgetary decisions, and does not provide incentives or tangible goals for achieving long-term deficit reduction. To address these concerns, some have recommended modifying the budget process in various ways to incorporate a long-term budgetary outlook.

Some critics of this approach, however, suggest that information already exists to make long-term evaluations possible, so that a shift to longer-term budgeting alone would not improve the ability of Congress or the President to make the decisions necessary to achieve long-term sustainability of budget policies. Further, some have argued that there are fundamental issues that make successful longer-term budgeting impractical, such as projection uncertainty, unforeseen events, and the problem of trying to bind future Congresses to specific goals.

President Obama's Commission on Fiscal Responsibility and Reform, several outside groups, and some members of Congress have released or are expected to release budget and budget process reform proposals. Many proposals contain reform options that focus on a longer-term outlook.

Five major proposals are analyzed in this report: (1) extending the time period of the current budget window to provide greater detail about fiscal challenges ahead and the long-term effects of proposed legislation; (2) employing multi-year budget controls that would require the outyears of the President's budget proposal and the congressional budget resolution to be adhered to; (3) creating annual fiscal targets that could be used either for informational purposes or to enforce specific budgetary outcomes; (4) increasing budget transparency in various ways; and (5) switching from cash-flow accounting to accrual-basis accounting to capture the effects of future entitlements in the current budget.

INTRODUCTION

Both the President and Congress play a role in forming federal spending and revenue policy: the President submits an annual budget proposal, and Congress typically adopts an annual budget resolution and then passes legislation, which must be signed by the President, within the parameters established by that budget resolution.[1]

These budgetary decisions, about overall federal spending and revenue, are currently made on an annual basis, and it has been argued that the process does not require or encourage the consideration of long-term concerns. Further, it has been argued that no uniform long-term goals exist for both the

President and Congress to work toward when designing their respective annual proposals.

Many groups and individuals, both inside and outside government, have been issuing recommendations to put the budget on a fiscal track that is sustainable over the long term. The budget is considered to be on a sustainable path if the resulting debt-to-GDP ratio is constant or falling. Some of these groups assert that to successfully make changes in spending and revenue policy, changes must be made to the budget process. They argue that the short-term focus of the current budget process has a dire effect on the long-term budget for several reasons: it allows difficult long-term decisions to be avoided; it hides the long-term effects of certain budgetary decisions; and it does not provide incentives or tangible goals for achieving long-term deficit reduction. To address these concerns, some have recommended modifying the budget process in various ways to focus on the long-term budgetary outlook.

This report will provide information on (1) the current horizons used in the budget process, including already existing long-term components; (2) the rationale for increased focus on longterm budgeting; (3) general challenges to long-term budgeting; and (4) an analysis of general proposals that have been made to increase the focus of long-term budgeting in the budget process. This report will not discuss general budget process reform proposals except those related to longterm budgeting, nor will it address policy proposals to reduce spending or increase revenues in the long run.[2] This report defines long-term budget process proposals to be those that affect the budget beyond the traditional five- or 10-year budget window.

Horizons Used in the Current Budget Process

The Traditional Five- or 10-Year Budget Horizons

With some exceptions, the budget window, as currently used in the federal budget process, typically spans either a five- or 10-year period. The purpose of the budget window and baseline projections is to evaluate how proposed legislation affects the current budget outlook and to measure whether legislation adheres to rules established by the House and Senate. The use of the 10-year budget window also balances the importance of considering both the current and future implications of budgetary decisions within the limits of constructing accurate and timely budget projections. Programs that may be manageable within the 10-year window may become unmanageable over a longer period, however.[3]

The annual baseline projection provided by the Congressional Budget Office (CBO) to assist Congress in decision making and budget enforcement spans 10 years. The CBO baseline projects federal spending and receipts under existing law as a benchmark for informational purposes, and for evaluating proposed budgetary changes in spending or revenue.[4] The CBO baseline has spanned a 10-year period since 1996; previously it spanned five years. The baseline is used by Congress as a starting point to construct the budget resolution.

The annual budget resolution, an agreement between the House and Senate used as an enforceable framework for annual budgetary decisions, requires a budget window of five years.[5] However, this requirement, from the Congressional Budget Act of 1974 (The Budget Act), is a minimum, and budget resolutions have occasionally spanned longer periods of time of up to 10 years.[6] In some fiscal years, when Congress does not reach an agreement on a budget resolution, spending and revenue decisions are not explicitly laid out.

In February of each year when the President submits his annual budget request encompassing his proposed policy changes, information is provided for a 10-year window. The Office of Management and Budget (OMB) prepares budget baselines that are included in the President's budget to illustrate the budgetary impact of his proposals. All of OMB's budget projections, the current law baseline, the current policy baseline, and the proposed policy projection, currently span a 10-year period.[7]

Within their respective budget proposals, both Congress and the President present budget goals they would like to achieve over the next five or 10 years. But since budget plans are revised annually, as a practical matter, the current budget process largely approaches spending and revenue decisions on an annual basis. The lack of a long-term focus in the budget process does not force action on already existing and well-known long-term fiscal issues.

CBO and the Joint Committee on Taxation (JCT) prepare spending and revenue estimates showing the budgetary impact of individual legislation to assist Congress in weighing the merits of a bill and for budget enforcement purposes. The Congressional Budget Act of 1974 requires that estimates apply to a five-year period, to ensure the measure's compliance with the budget resolution.[8] Estimates, however, frequently span other time periods to assist with enforcement of other budgetary rules.

The House and Senate each have PAYGO rules with the parallel goal of ensuring deficit neutrality of any new direct spending or revenue legislation, based on the CBO or JCT score of the legislation.[9] The House and Senate PAYGO rules cover a six-year and an 11-year period. To enforce PAYGO rules, a member must raise a point of order, which can be waived by a majority vote in the House or a three-fifths vote in the Senate. As with all House rules, the PAYGO rule in the House must be re-adopted in each new Congress; the Senate PAYGO rule is currently set to expire in 2017.

Additionally, there is a statutory PAYGO requirement that applies to both a five-year and a 10- year period.[10] Statutory PAYGO, as enacted in February 2010, seeks to enforce deficit neutrality on the net impact of new revenue and mandatory (direct) spending provisions by recording their budgetary effects on two scorecards maintained by OMB covering rolling five- and 10-year periods. After the conclusion of a congressional session, if a debit has been recorded for the budget year on either scorecard the President issues a sequestration order that implements across-the-board cuts in non-exempt direct spending programs by an amount sufficient to rectify the debit on the PAYGO scorecard. Amending statutory PAYGO would require the enactment of new legislation. Generally, House and Senate PAYGO rules seek to enforce deficit neutrality on individual legislation; statutory PAYGO seeks to enforce deficit neutrality on overall mandatory spending and revenue legislation enacted over the entire session.

Existing Long-Term Budgeting Components

Some components of the budget process already deal with long-term budget issues. This means that data already exist, in publicly available formats, to assist in evaluating the country's longterm fiscal health. In some instances, data evaluating the long-term outlook of certain programs are currently available, including on those programs which are generally thought of as the most challenging to deal with going forward. Long-term components of the budget process can be separated into two general categories and are currently used for two distinct purposes: long-term budgetary data used for informational purposes and rules affecting long-term outcomes that are used for enforcement purposes.

Informational Components

Generally, long-term informational components are used, not to enforce specific outcomes, but to provide budgetary information to assist with congressional decision making. Several government publications already provide long-term budget projections and options for reducing the budget deficit to a sustainable level. However, only OMB's long-term projections are included in the primary budget documents, and OMB's projections are presented in a different volume from the main proposal.

Since 1996, the CBO has periodically published *The Long-Term Budget Outlook*, which "presents illustrative scenarios for federal spending and revenues and describes the implications of those scenarios for the economy."[11] One goal of the report is to provide information on the long-term budgetary pressures associated with the aging of the baby-boom generation and the continued growth in healthcare costs. The current report mainly focuses on projections out to 2035, with additional data to 2084 available in the "Data Underlying Scenarios and Figures" posted on the CBO website. Projections of revenue, spending, and federal debt are made under several different scenarios because of the uncertainty related to budgetary and economic assumptions. The report also presents estimates of the "fiscal gap," which is the amount that spending must be permanently cut or revenues must be permanently raised to stabilize the debt as a share of GDP over the long run.

Similarly, the "Long Term Budget Outlook" chapter of the *Analytical Perspectives* volume of the President's Budget includes 75-year projections for current programs. These projections are based on a variety of variables, including long-range cost projections from the Centers for Medicare and Medicaid Services. This section also incorporates demographic and economic assumptions and illustrates alternative spending, revenue, and growth scenarios. The Government Accountability Office (GAO) also produces a similar report on the long-term budget outlook using their own models and simulations.[12] CBO, OMB, and GAO all agree that the budget is on an unsustainable path, largely driven by the projected long-term growth in Medicare, Medicaid, and Social Security, which is not matched by projected growth in revenues.

Social Security and Medicare Trustees issue respective actuarial estimates of each trust fund for the upcoming 75-year period.[13] These reports contain both short- and long-range projections of annual program expenditures and payroll tax receipts. There are also estimates of the actuarial deficits over the next 75 years that measure the solvency of the trust funds relative to dedicated revenues. These deficits represent the shortfall between the program's projected expenditures and income. The Trustees' reports do not address how these programs affect the sustainability of the overall budget.

Finally, another comprehensive look at the financial outlook is contained in the Department of the Treasury report *Financial Report of the United States Government.*[14] This report uses accrual-based accounting methods to present a balance sheet for the federal government. It includes certain liabilities of the government on a net present value basis, including federal employee and veteran benefits, and federal insurance and loan guarantee liabilities. This report does not treat the future projected shortfalls of Social Security and Medicare to be official liabilities of the government, but provides estimates of the long-term actuarial deficits of the programs nevertheless.

Enforcement Components

The long-term reports discussed in the previous section do not play a role in current enforcement mechanisms. Most existing enforcement mechanisms, like PAYGO or the levels in the budget resolution, apply to shorter budget windows, with some exceptions.

In the Senate, it is not in order to consider a reconciliation measure that would increase the deficit or reduce the surplus outside the budget window provided in the budget resolution.[15] In addition, it is not in order to consider a measure that would cause a net increase in the deficit in excess of $5 billion in any of the four 10-year periods beginning in 2019 through 2058.[16] Both of these rules can be waived by a three-fifths vote of all Senators duly chosen and sworn.

In the House, it is not in order to consider legislation that would provide for a net increase in Social Security benefits or decrease in Social Security taxes in excess of 0.02% of the present value of future taxable payroll for a 75-year period, or in excess of $250 million for the first five-year period after it becomes effective.[17] In addition, it is not in order in the House to consider legislation that would cause a net increase in mandatory spending in excess of $5 billion in any of the four consecutive 10-year periods following the budget window included in the latest congressional budget resolution.[18] These points of order can be waived by a simple majority.[19]

THE RATIONALE FOR LONG-TERM BUDGETING

Large budget deficits have persisted over the past several fiscal years. Federal debt held by the public as a percentage of gross domestic product (GDP) has risen from 36% in 2007, prior to the current economic downturn, to roughly 62% as of the end of 2010.[20] Deficits at current levels are considered unsustainable because they are large enough to cause the debt to continually rise relative to GDP, and are projected to grow larger beyond the 10-year budget window. Under one set of policy assumptions, debt held by the public as a percentage of GDP is projected to rise to nearly 90% by 2020 and 185% by 2035.[21] If this were to actually occur, the accumulating debt would lead to significant growth in net interest payments, crowding out of other types of investment, reduced national savings, increased interest rates, a reduction in the flexibility of policymakers to handle unexpected challenges, and an increased likelihood of a fiscal crisis.

The short-term focus of the current process arguably obscures the long-term effects of the growth of certain programs, and it does not highlight potentially difficult long-term tradeoffs. Further, it does not provide incentives or tangible goals for achieving long-term deficit reduction. Since delay increases the size of the fiscal imbalance, critics argue that this exacerbates a long-term outlook that is already unsustainable, and that it is easier to solve long-term problems ahead of time than if decisions are postponed. Making changes earlier allows changes to be phased in more gradually and allows those that cannot adjust to changes to be exempted. For example, if policymakers decided to reduce entitlement benefits for the elderly, a longer phase-in period would make it easier to exempt from the changes those who are already retired (and cannot earn or save more to compensate).

The 10-year window for scoring legislation, and its interaction with existing enforcement mechanisms, provides an incentive to make legislation less costly within the 10-year window than outside of it. This encourages the use of phased-in provisions or provisions that reduce the deficit in the short run but increase the deficit in the long run. For example, the creation of Roth Individual Retirement Accounts (IRAs) as an alternative to traditional IRAs raises revenues in the short run, because taxes on Roth IRAs are paid at the time of contribution, but loses revenues in the long run, when accumulated growth is exempt from tax.

An alternative perspective on long-term budgeting posits that the nation's long-term fiscal problems are already well understood, potential solutions are already well chronicled, and the specific problems are unrelated to the long-term budget information. Nor has deficit reduction been ignored in the current budget—for example, a central goal in the President's budget proposal for the past two fiscal years has been to reduce the deficit over the budget window, and the Administration has made specific proposals on how to achieve that goal—although it has not yet been accomplished. A case can be made that the main problem with tackling fiscal sustainability is that current policy for revenue and mandatory spending (which comprises approximately three-fifths of total spending) is automatic and will continue at levels inconsistent with sustainability. A shift to long-term budgeting alone would not change this fact. From this perspective, changes in the budget process are secondary to the problem of arriving at consensus on the changes to revenues or spending necessary to provide sustainability. That is, budget process reform can not be a substitute for the tough decisions required on long-term spending and revenue policy in order to reach fiscal sustainability.

Furthermore, since the current fiscal year's deficit is already large, addressing the budget deficit "problem" does not require detailed knowledge of the long-term budget outlook, nor does it require incorporation of the long-term budget into the budget process. Since the current five- to 10-year budget windows used for planning and enforcement mechanisms have been unsuccessful in reducing budget deficits over the next five to 10 years to sustainable levels, would a longer budget window be successful in solving long-term fiscal issues? Some feel that while many types of budget process reform could be useful, "the process is not the problem. The problem is the problem."[22]

MAJOR CHALLENGES ASSOCIATED WITH LONG-TERM BUDGETING

If Congress were to adopt a budget process with an increased long-term focus, there are several challenges to address when shaping changes. These include addressing the automatic nature of most mandatory spending and revenue, projection uncertainty, unforeseen events, underlying projection assumptions, and the problem of trying to bind future Congresses or the President to Congress's current goals. In addition, determining how to integrate information for purposes of enforcing budgetary goals may be difficult.

The Automatic Nature of Most Mandatory Spending and Revenue

Mandatory spending currently makes up about three-fifths of total federal spending. Most of it is automatic, that is, it does not require congressional action to continue in the current form. Examples of mandatory programs include Medicare and Medicaid, where benefits are paid out if an individual meets the eligibility criteria, and interest paid on the federal debt. Further, these programs are the ones that are forecast to grow most rapidly in the long run. Because spending on these programs occurs unless new legislation changes the benefit structure or eligibility criteria, changes to the budget process to incorporate long-term decisions are unlikely to restore sustainability unless they incorporate a way to deal with the "autopilot" spending that occurs under these programs. Likewise, most components of the tax code are permanent, and there is no mechanism in place to require Congress to adjust them if current revenue levels are inconsistent with long-term goals. Some major provisions do have sunset provisions, but depending on these opportunities alone could lead to any needed revenue adjustments being concentrated in only those parts of the tax code that require extension.

Of course, the fact that most mandatory spending and revenue laws are permanent could be seen as a form of long-term budgeting. But in the context of the current long-term fiscal imbalance, the problem with the permanent nature of these programs is that because the formulas that determine spending and revenue are fixed, so is the imbalance.

Projection Uncertainty

Using long-term projections as a base for budgetary decisions can be problematic. Projections of any type contain a degree of uncertainty. The further out a projection is relative to when it is made, the more inaccurate it tends to be. Budget baseline estimates and projections are highly sensitive to small changes in underlying assumptions and economic factors, and changes to these assumptions grow in importance as the forecast is extended. Economic forecasts remain subject to substantial margins of error, even over short periods of time. Although cyclical factors even out over time, small errors in underlying structural factors can compound to cause large differences in long-term totals. Making programmatic changes to achieve fiscal goals based on these projections may result in changes that ultimately over- or under-shoot what is needed. For example, based on past forecast errors, CBO has estimated that there is a 50% chance that the budget deficit will be 0.5 percentage points of GDP higher or lower than their January projection for the current year, and 2.2 percentage points of GDP higher or lower for five years in the future.[23]

Unforeseen Events

Most of the legislative spending increases relative to the baseline that occurred in the past decade were due to unforeseen events, including the terrorist attacks of September 11, 2001, military outlays in Afghanistan and Iraq, Hurricane Katrina and other natural disasters, and the 2008 financial crisis. Spending has increased significantly over the past several fiscal years due to the economic downturn and resulting legislation. At the same time, revenues have also declined, resulting in large budget deficits. Unexpected shocks like these, which led to the large increases in spending and declines in revenues, are unpredictable and would be difficult to account for in a long-term budget process. Over long periods of time, events are even harder to predict—75 years ago, the nation was in the midst of the Great Depression, had not yet fought World War II, and major federal programs such as Medicare and Medicaid did not exist. Inserting flexible mechanisms to deal with uncertain situations and "emergencies" as they occur may be necessary, but risk compromising the ability to achieve the overall goals of a long-term budget process.

Underlying Projection Assumptions

Budget projections are based on simple rules of thumb, where more sophisticated projections are impractical. In long-term budget projections, these rules of thumb include assuming discretionary spending remains constant as a share of GDP, revenues stay constant as a share of GDP (in some projections), and that health spending will initially grow faster than GDP based on historical rates, but gradually grow no faster than GDP. Small changes to these rules of thumb lead to large differences in outcomes over 75 years. For example, CBO projects that federal spending on healthcare will rise from 5.5% of GDP in 2010 to 10.9% of GDP in 2035. But if healthcare spending grows more closely to historical rates, federal healthcare spending would be 11.5% of GDP in 2035, and if healthcare spending grows at the same rates as GDP, federal healthcare spending would be 8.7% of GDP in 2035.

Another challenge posed by incorporating long-term projections into official projections is that current rules of thumb in the official baseline are different than those used in long-term projections. This is because simple extrapolations of the 10-year baseline would lead to results that bear no relationship to current policy over 75 years. In the official 10-year baseline, these rules of thumb include adjusting discretionary spending for inflation, and allowing tax provisions to expire as scheduled, including the 2001 to 2003 tax cuts (popularly referred to as "Bush tax cuts") and the inflation adjustment to the alternative minimum tax (AMT). If those rules of thumb were used over 75 years, discretionary spending would fall to a share of GDP much smaller than historical levels and most taxpayers would fall under the AMT by the end of the projection period.

Binding Future Congresses or the President to Congress's Goals

Another challenge to long-term budgeting is the difficulty of the current Congress to bind future Congresses to its plans. Congress may set detailed plans for changes to be made to future spending programs and the tax code that restore solvency, but even if these changes are enacted into law, future Congresses would be free to change them.

There is also no guarantee that Congress and the President will agree on overall goals, or specific ways to meet them, either now or in the future. Without uniform annual or long-term objectives in the budget process, both the President and Congress lack shared goals to work towards when designing the President's budget proposal or the congressional budget resolution. If the President and Congress disagree on goals, each side may lack the incentive to take steps necessary to meet their respective goals.

Analysis of Long-Term Budgeting Proposals

Congressional interest in budget reform has grown in light of current and forecast budget deficits as well as increasing public concern over the long-term budget outlook. President Obama's National Commission on Fiscal Responsibility and Reform, several outside groups, and some members of Congress have released or are expected to release proposals with the goal of returning the federal budget to a more sustainable course. Some proposals contain options to reform the budget process with an emphasis on changing the budgetary focus to a more long-term outlook. To implement a viable long-term budget process, it would be important to incorporate both information and enforcement mechanisms into changes to budget procedure.

As discussed above, the current budget process has been criticized on three grounds in relation to the current budget window. It allows difficult long-term decisions to be avoided, it hides the longterm effects of certain budgetary decisions, and it does not provide incentives or tangible goals for achieving long-term deficit reduction. The following sections evaluate proposals that attempt to address these issues. Those proposals include extending the current budget window, adopting a multi-year budget process, creating statutory deficit targets, switching from cash-flow accounting to accrual-basis accounting, and increasing the transparency of budget decisions. In many cases, these proposals have been discussed in general terms with limited detail.

Extend the Current Budget Window

Certain proposals recommend extending the current five- or 10-year budget window, to encompass a greater period of time, such as 20 years. It has been asserted that this will not only provide greater detail about the fiscal challenges that lie ahead but also provide information on the effects that proposed legislation may have beyond the five- or 10-year budget period. As discussed earlier, the current budget window essentially ignores the effects of spending and revenue provisions on the fiscal outlook. This means that neither the impact of new legislation nor the performance of current programs beyond the 10-year period is generally available for consideration during votes.[24] Further, programs like Social Security, whose finances are not necessarily out of balance in the short run, have well-discussed long-term imbalances. Currently, budget enforcement mechanisms, like statutory PAYGO, examine the effects of new provisions on the baseline over the next five or 10 years and evaluate whether or not they meet specific goals over that period.

To improve the long-term fiscal outlook, it may be necessary to know how new legislation or programmatic changes, reforms, or modifications affect the budget beyond the current decade. This would require budget projections to extend into a second decade or beyond. Because there is a significant degree of uncertainty associated with projections, especially beyond the first 10 years, proposing to extend the budget window should proceed with some caution.

Further, even if the budget window were to be extended to 20 or 30 years, it may still be possible to hide the costs of certain obligations or the long-term costs of certain programs even beyond that period of time.

Incorporating projections beyond 10 years into the budget process could be useful for informational purposes, which may not necessarily be tied to enforcement. OMB, CBO, and Treasury already produce information out 75 years that could be used in an extended budget window. CBO could also include this information in their cost estimates of legislation.

Adopt Multi-Year Budget Plans

Budget reform advocates often include proposals for a multi-year budget plan that they assert would help reach long-term budgetary goals. The annual budget resolution already requires a budget window containing spending, revenue, and deficit levels for the upcoming fiscal year and the following four years. Similarly, the President already submits a budget proposal that covers multiple years. These budgets, however, are resubmitted annually with multi-year information revised each year. For instance, a budget resolution for FY2011 may include a spending level for FY2012, but the following year when the budget resolution for FY2012 is drafted, it need not adhere to the FY2012 levels set in the prior year's budget resolution. So while each budget includes outyears, those levels can be altered from year to year.

In contrast to current practice, proposals for multi-year budget plans would require that budget levels remain consistent from year to year. It has been proposed that this be achieved by creating a multi-year budget process. (It has also been suggested that this be achieved by setting deficit or debt targets each year, as discussed in the next section.) According to a generic multi-year budget plan, the President would submit a multi-year budget proposal every two or more years and Congress would no longer adopt a budget resolution annually but instead adopt a budget resolution every few years. Under some proposals, appropriation bills could also cover multiple years. By doing this, it is argued that Congress would agree upon future year limits and be forced to adhere to them.

Traditionally, advocates for biennial or multi-year budgeting assert that it would lighten the congressional workload because Congress would no longer need to make budgetary decisions annually, allowing more time to focus on other matters, such as executive branch oversight and budgetary planning. This argument was particularly prevalent in years when the budget resolution was not agreed to or was agreed to later than expected. More recently, multi-year budgeting has been viewed as a tool for setting and adhering to medium and long-term deficit goals.

Some critics feel that it unrealistic to expect one Congress to agree to adhere to a budget set by a previous Congress, given that policy priorities change and unexpected contingencies arise. This applies not just to an overall budgetary goal, but also to individual components of the budget.

Multi-year budgets could also reduce the effectiveness of program implementation. Under the current annual budget process, a significant period of time already elapses between when agencies request funding for specific activities, and when Congress actually considers such legislation. For example, work on the President's FY2012 budget began in the summer of 2010 as agencies began to develop their budget requests. Under proposed plans for multi-year budgeting, the budget resolution would give committees their allocations for the next few years and would require the executive agencies to assess their future needs even further in advance.

Further, binding a Congress to previously agreed-to totals could result in avoidance and accounting gimmickry. For example, if a multi-year budget allowed emergency spending above the planned total, there would be incentive to classify any proposal as emergency to avoid budget caps. Reducing the frequency of aggregate budget decisions, as would occur under multi-year budgeting, may "raise the stakes" during decision making and may increase the likelihood of contention and delay—the opposite outcome of one traditional rationale for multi-year budgeting.

One logistical issue to note with multi-year budgeting is that all rules in the House, including a budget resolution, must be re-affirmed as the House reconstitutes itself at the beginning of a new Congress. This would mean that a budget resolution agreed to in the prior Congress would have to be agreed to again by the new House. If a future House of Representatives did not agree with the budgetary goals set by the previous, there is no way to compel their adherence. This makes it difficult to switch to more than a biennial budget process.

Create Deficit or Debt Targets

Many long-term budget reform proposals include budget deficit or debt targets that would reach into the long term. This would require Congress and the President to submit budget proposals that adhere to those targets. In designing a target, there are several features to consider.

Type of Target

Perhaps the first question is whether targets should be set in dollar terms or as a percentage of GDP. Economically, GDP targets are more meaningful because a larger economy is less affected by any given dollar amount of debt. Further, if the target covers an extended period of time, projection error is more of a problem for a dollar target than a GDP target. For example, lower than expected inflation over an extended period of time would make a dollar target more onerous in real terms, and vice versa. Procedurally, the current budget system revolves around dollar totals, so a GDP target might add complexity to the current process. Another disadvantage to GDP targets is that data are frequently revised and available with a lag. The plan would need to take into account that a target that is met before a data revision could turn out to be missed after the revision. A hybrid system, where long-term goals are expressed as a percentage of GDP, but totals for the current year are converted into dollars each year, might address some of these issues.

Second, should the target be set in terms of the publicly held debt or the unified budget deficit?[25] In a broad sense, the distinction is not important, since deficits lead to nearly one-to-one changes in the publicly held debt. But if the plan contains only a final target, without interim targets, a debt target would require that higher than expected deficits in some years be negated by lower deficits in other years. Annual targets, in contrast, would presumably allow bygones to be bygones—a higher than expected deficit in the previous year would not change the deficit target for the current year. If debt is targeted as a share of GDP, it would also allow larger deficits relative to GDP when the economy is growing faster, for better or worse, since a larger GDP could accommodate a larger debt buildup along the way to the target.

Third, should targets be agreed upon by both Congress and the Administration, perhaps through the enactment of legislation? Enacting statutory fiscal goals to guide these budgetary decisions may create a national coherence in budgetary decision making that would lead to a more forward-looking long-term budget outlook. Further, it would emphasize the expectation that both the President and Congress are working toward a long-term solution to address the expected growth in the national debt. Under such a proposal, Congress and the President could agree on just a deficit target, leaving both free in the future to advocate different ways to reach that target, or they could agree on more detailed spending and revenue proposals to meet that target up front. A drawback of this approach is that if Congress and the Administration reach an impasse in setting the goals, progress toward deficit reduction could cease. If Congress worked toward deficit reduction alone, the President could only stop it through the use of the veto.

Fourth, how ambitious should the deficit or debt targets be? Some state that the targets should be modest and gradual so that they will be easier to achieve and therefore more effective over the long term. Advocates of modest targets state that more ambitious targets lead to the use of accounting gimmicks because they are otherwise impossible to meet. Additionally, it has been argued that the difficulty of reaching ambitious targets will require them to be modified later on. For instance, the deficit targets set under Gramm-Rudman-Hollings in 1985 were revised upward by the Balanced Budget and Emergency Deficit Control Reaffirmation Act of 1987 (1987 Reaffirmation Act). The 1987 Reaffirmation Act extended by two years the time frame set out in the 1985 act for achieving a balanced budget, requiring a balanced budget by FY1993 instead of FY1991. (In reality, the budget was not in surplus until 1998.)

Advocates of more ambitious targets claim that they are needed given the size of the fiscal imbalance. They assert that smaller, more gradual changes are a disadvantage because they require only some programs to suffer, and without shared sacrifice, any changes in spending or revenue are less politically palatable. Another argument is that overly modest goals just lead to a patchwork of smaller legislative changes and that an accumulation of this creates complicated, incoherent policy. Instead, it is argued that comprehensive changes need to be made all at once to ensure significant savings and good policy.

Finally, would Congress adopt a final target to be reached by the end of the budget window, or would there be interim targets that must be met in each year of the plan? A final target gives policymakers more flexibility to react to unforeseen contingencies and adjust the budget to take them into account. For example, in response to a natural disaster, policymakers might decide to raise the deficit that year, and then find additional savings in future years to ensure that the ultimate target is still met. On the other hand, annual targets make it more likely that the plan "stays on track," and policymakers do not procrastinate on changes until it is too late. That is, earlier Congresses may have little incentive to work toward a final target that applies only to later Congresses. Proposals to set statutory annual targets are discussed in more detail below.

Setting Statutory Annual Targets

A proposal to create annual deficit targets would require the President to submit a budget consistent with these goals. Additionally, when crafting a budget resolution, the House and Senate budget committees would determine the amount of savings needed to reach the annual fiscal target based on the baseline projection provided by the CBO. The budget resolution would then set aggregate spending and revenue levels consistent with the savings needed, and would make committee allocations (referred to as 302(a) allocations) that would fulfill the requirements associated with spending. The targets could be enforced by creating a point of order in the House and Senate that would disallow the floor consideration of a budget resolution that did not adhere to the prescribed deficit levels. It is unclear how an annual target would be achieved in years when Congress does not adopt a budget resolution.

Congress may also wish to consider under what circumstances the annual targets could be waived or modified. The target could be waived in specific circumstances designated ahead of time such as war or recession, or Congress could be given the discretion to waive it. Instead of mandating the use of precise deficit targets, setting a longer-term goal, with interim annual goals to be used as benchmarks to meet it, may be more flexible and easy to enforce. If, in any year, the annual goals are not reached due to incorrect economic or technical assumptions used to make projections, the next year's annual target could be revised to keep the budget on track to meet the longer-term target. If strong economic performance accelerates the time table whereby the longer-term target could be met, the target could be revised. Setting a longer-term target with somewhat flexible intermediate goals could be more accommodating in terms of handling the effects of the business cycle. On the other hand, flexibility on interim targets could undermine the ultimate goal if it is used as a way to avoid taking unpopular steps.

Enforcement Mechanisms for Annual Deficit Targets

Statutory deficit levels, such as those described above, could exist solely for informational and guidance purposes, or they could include enforcement mechanisms, which would require that specified goals be met. Enforcement could be viewed as a spectrum of severity. At the least severe end of the spectrum, the targets could be enacted as a way of agreeing on long-term national goals. Some believe that this type of enforcement mechanism would suffice because the public's expectations would compel the President and Congress to adhere to the set levels. On the other hand, others assert that without an explicit enforcement mechanism, levels will easily be ignored, particularly during difficult domestic periods.

In a more severe form, these targets could either be enforced through congressional points of order on the floor, or they could be enforced by a statutory mechanism, such as sequestration, which would make automatic, across-the-board cuts to non-exempt spending programs when levels are breached. The sequestration process has been used historically in the budget process in several forms.

Arguably, using only congressional points of order as enforcement mechanisms may not be adequate because points of order can be waived. In addition, future Congresses may choose to waive or modify the rules that create these points of order. Further, if adhering to the annual deficit targets would require new legislation to make changes in mandatory (direct) spending or revenue, there is no way to compel the creation of this legislation through points of order. Instead, additional provisions would need to be included, most likely as expedited congressional procedures, that would attempt to force Congress to vote on a package of legislative changes.[26] However, forcing Congress to consider, and further, to agree by a certain time on the spending or revenue changes necessary to meet the targets is logistically difficult. The reconciliation process already exists to facilitate that process. The reconciliation process as established by the Budget Act facilitates the changing of existing spending, revenue, and debt-limit laws to bring them into compliance with current fiscal priorities established in the annual budget resolution. One of the many unique features of the reconciliation process is expedited floor procedures.[27] Reconciliation has been used in the past to achieve significant deficit reduction.[28]

Some argue that congressional points of order and expedited procedures may be a safer enforcement mechanism because the levels could be waived by Congress when emergency situations occur and it is advantageous to have the option of breaching statutory levels. However, past enforcement mechanisms, like sequestration, have provided some flexibility for specific economic and domestic situations. For instance, the deficit reduction procedures included in The Balanced Budget and Emergency Deficit Control Act of 1985 (Gramm-Rudman-Hollings; P.L. 99-177) allowed for suspension in wartime and in the event of a recession. If real economic growth was projected to be negative in two consecutive quarters, or if the Commerce Department reported that actual real growth was below 1% in two consecutive quarters, the deficit level provisions could be suspended. In such an event, Congress could consider a joint resolution under expedited procedures, that once enacted would suspend the deficit reduction provisions for the current fiscal year or for all fiscal years.

Sequestration has existed as an enforcement mechanism in several forms in connection with budget and budget process reform. For instance, it was part of Gramm-Rudman-Hollings in 1985 and continued in some form until 2002 (as described below). Sequestration is currently used to enforce Statutory PAYGO. Within Statutory PAYGO, budgetary effects of new enacted direct spending and revenue provisions are recorded on two separate scorecards. At the end of a congressional session, the scorecards are evaluated to determine if a debit has been recorded for the current budget year; that is, if new legislation has increased or created a deficit. If no such debit is found, no action occurs. If a debit is found, however, the President must issue a sequestration order which automatically implements across-the-board cuts to non-exempt direct spending programs to compensate for the amount of the debit.

Although it has been widely asserted that the mere threat of a sequester forces action, that has been disputed by those who witnessed sequestration under Gramm-Rudman-Hollings. They state that the threat of across-the-board cuts is potentially less politically painful than having to vote on specific spending cuts. Further, many have argued that the threat of sequestration becomes less alarming if more prominent programs are exempt. More information about programs exempt from sequestration is included in the section below.

As seen under previous budget process reforms, projection errors over the span of the year mean that good faith attempts to reach deficit targets can be undermined by events outside congressional control. In particular, only the levels of spending for discretionary programs are determined directly by Congress. Revenue and mandatory spending levels are determined by the interaction between the formulas laid out in statute and the changing circumstances that make individuals liable or eligible, respectively, under that formula. For example, it may be that significant legislation has been enacted to put the country on track to meet the annual deficit target based on certain projections and assumptions used at the time. However, by the end of the year, the original projections may end up being inaccurate, perhaps because the economy did not function as expected, leading to a deficit target that was not reached. In such cases, enforcement could be automatically applied once the projection has been revised, requiring additional actions when the deficit is larger than projected, or enforcement could be applied only to the levels contained in the original budget resolution (based on the original projection), allowing the target to be missed.

Parts of the Budget Subject to an Enforcement Mechanism

If a deficit target applies to the budget as a whole, which includes the components of (1) discretionary spending, (2) mandatory spending, and (3) revenue, will the enforcement mechanism also apply to all components? And will it apply proportionately? Gramm-Rudman-Hollings included general deficit targets that applied to the budget as a whole and were enforced by sequestration, applying formulaic cuts to discretionary and direct spending programs. Controversy arose as many felt that the inability to achieve the deficit targets was caused by changing projections of the impact of revenues or direct spending on the deficit even when action had already been taken to reduce discretionary spending. These criticisms led to the Budget Enforcement Act of 1990 (BEA), which created a "firewall" between discretionary spending and direct spending.[29] Caps were set for discretionary spending and were enforced by sequestration solely to discretionary spending programs. PAYGO was established to enforce deficit reductions achieved by changes to revenues and direct spending enacted through reconciliation by limiting the ability of Congress to enact new direct spending and revenue legislation and was enforced by sequestration.

Budget enforcement mechanisms, such as sequestration, frequently focus only on spending and not on revenue. This characteristic of budgetary enforcement has also been criticized as being unattractive. For example, if revenue decreases occur over the course of a year, either due to changes in law or economic factors, some believe it is not fair that spending should absorb the resultant impact on the deficit. Therefore, proposals have been made that a sequester should be accompanied by an automatic revenue surcharge. A mechanism that would apply to all components of the budget, and do so proportionately, would need to be very sophisticated and would likely require alterations over the long term.

Although across-the-board enforcement mechanisms have been criticized for their formulaic and indiscriminate manner of making cuts, they can be tailored to exempt or shield certain programs, making the process more discriminate but greatly reducing the effectiveness as a tool for deficit reduction. For example, under Statutory PAYGO, certain programs and activities are exempt from the PAYGO scorecards, including provisions deemed an emergency by Congress and provisions dealing with four specific "current policy" areas. The four specified areas are Medicare physicians' payments, the estate and gift tax, the alternative minimum tax (AMT), and extension of certain income tax cuts for the middle class enacted in 2001 and

2003. Without these exemptions, offsets of over $200 billion could be required in 2011 to finance them.

Additionally, certain programs have been exempt from sequestration itself. Under Statutory PAYGO some direct spending programs and activities are exempt from sequestration, such as Social Security and Tier I Railroad Retirement benefits, federal employee retirement and disability programs, Supplemental Security Income (SSI), Supplemental Nutrition Assistance Program (SNAP), Children's Health Insurance Program (CHIP), Temporary Assistance for Needy Families (TANF), veterans' programs, net interest, refundable income tax credits, Medicaid, and unemployment compensation. In 2010, these exemptions amounted to roughly half of total federal spending. In addition, sequestration, or any enforcement mechanism, can be tailored not only to exempt certain programs, but in some instances to at least shield non-exempt programs. For example, a previous form of sequestration limited reductions in Medicare to 4%.

Switch from Cash-Flow Accounting to Accrual-Basis Accounting

Outlays and revenues are primarily recorded in primary federal budget documents on a cash-flow basis: expenditures are recorded in the fiscal year they are paid out and revenues are recorded in the year they are received.[30] For entitlement programs, this means that benefits that have already been promised are not recorded in the budget until the year they are paid out; and there is no record of benefits in the budget in the year they accrue. Critics argue that cash-flow budgeting hides the impact of entitlement programs for the elderly on long-term fiscal solvency (notably, Social Security, Medicare, and parts of Medicaid) since those programs currently have a cash-flow surplus but are projected to face much larger cash-flow deficits in the future.

As discussed above, the primary source of the projected long-term fiscal imbalance is arguably the growth in elderly entitlement spending without a corresponding increase in overall revenues. One method for capturing the effects of future entitlement growth on the current budget would be to switch from cash-flow accounting to accrual-basis accounting. Instead of recording obligations as they are paid out, accrual-based accounting would record the net-present value of obligations as they are incurred.[31] Under this method, the difference between the present value of newly accrued future benefits and the present value of newly collected receipts (in the case of Social Security and Medicare, payroll taxes) would be recorded as net expenditures.[32] New benefit obligations accrue on an annual basis both because newly covered workers enter the entitlement systems and because existing covered workers accrue additional future benefits.

As a comparison, accrual-basis accounting is generally used by private corporations to record future pension and health benefits legally promised to workers. The case for private corporations to use accrual-basis accounting is more clear cut, however, since private corporations cannot generally alter legally guaranteed benefits once they have been contracted. The government, on the other hand, can legislate changes to benefits at any time, and has done so in the past. Accrual-basis accounting requires corporations to hold financial assets to back future benefits that have accrued in order to maintain the solvency of corporate benefit plans. If deficits in corporate plans become too large (when benefits prove to be higher than forecast or asset returns prove to be lower than forecast), accounting rules require that these deficits be made up over a designated period of time by the corporation increasing the assets backing the plans. By contrast, a shift to accrual-basis accounting in the federal budget may—but need not—be accompanied by a requirement that the government begin to hold assets to back accrued future benefits. Therefore, a shift to accrual-basis budgeting alone, without any other changes to entitlement programs, would not change the government's current or future fiscal imbalance. Alternatively, the government could choose to begin to require that assets be held to back future benefits without adopting accrual-basis budgeting.

Proponents of accrual-basis accounting would argue that it would make the fiscal imbalance more visible and may increase political pressure to address the imbalance. In particular, a shift to accrual-basis budgeting would shift the existing imbalance within entitlement programs for the elderly (between future promised benefits and future dedicated revenue from payroll taxes) from the future to the present budget. The shortfall between the income and expenditures of current and past participants in Social Security is $17.5 trillion in present value terms, according to the Social Security trustees. For Medicare Part A, the shortfall is $6.9 trillion in present value terms. For Medicare Part B, the shortfall is $10.6 trillion in present value terms, which under current law would be made up through general revenues.

There are a number of drawbacks to a shift to accrual-basis accounting. First, from an economic perspective, cash-basis accounting arguably best reflects the effect of the current budget deficit on the current economy because it most closely matches the actual funds that the government must borrow at any given time. By contrast, under accrual-basis budgeting, the federal debt (excluding the intergovernmental debt) would no longer match the actual liabilities of the federal government held by the public, and the budget deficit would no longer match the incremental increase in that debt. This result may also reduce the transparency of the overall budget, even as it increases the transparency of the imbalance in future entitlements. Second, accrual-basis accounting is potentially more subject to manipulation because net expenditures depend heavily on what assumptions are made about demographic factors, such as life expectancy; discount rates; economic factors, such as the growth in future covered wages; and future rates of return on assets held (if any) to back future benefits. All of these factors are subject to uncertainty, yet if more favorable assumptions in any of these areas are used, it would make the current budget balance more favorable.

An argument could be made that accrual-basis budgeting is unnecessary because the long-term fiscal imbalance is already well known, much debated, and captured in other official measures, such as the long-term budget projections prepared by CBO and OMB described above. In addition, accrual-based estimates are already available in the *Financial Report of the United States Government*, although it does not formally incorporate elderly entitlement programs as liabilities on the government balance sheet.[33] As discussed, these long-term budget projections do not play a formal role in the congressional budget process and are not used in current enforcement mechanisms, however.

A switch to accrual-basis accounting raises some technical questions. How would the transition from cash-basis accounting be accomplished? In order to make comparisons over time, would historical budgets be revised on an accrual basis? If not, how would future benefits that were accrued in past fiscal years be recorded? To deal with the shortcomings outlined above, would the government present two sets of books, one cash basis and one accrual basis? If so, how would this affect comprehension of budget issues for both policymakers and the public? Would the government switch to a system that was entirely accrual-basis, or a hybrid system where entitlement programs for the elderly are recorded on an accrual basis and the rest of the budget is calculated on a cash-flow basis? If so, how would this affect transparency?

Increase the Transparency of Budgetary Decisions

Increasing budget transparency does not directly lead to fiscal sustainability. It may, however, provide greater understanding of long-term challenges and greater incentives for Congress and the President to pursue and adhere to specific long-term debt reduction goals. According to this argument, if current budgetary information did not obscure the size and nature of the long-term fiscal imbalance, there would be greater public support for a solution and more public pressure on policymakers to reach a consensus on a solution.

One option is to make existing long-term budget information more prominent or require it to be included in budget presentations. Many of the other long-term budget proposals discussed in this report, including a longer budget or scoring window, prominent debt or deficit targets agreed upon by the President and Congress, and a switch to accrual accounting, would help further transparency in terms of making information more prominent and central to the budget process. On the other hand, certain long-term budgeting concepts such as the fiscal gap and accrual accounting are highly complex, and could decrease transparency in terms of public understanding of the issue.

Another option would be to require the President to address the nation in a public forum, such as an annual address to Congress, detailing the progress toward achieving fiscal targets or other long-term goals. Such an address could also lay out plans for how to continue to achieve these goals over the next several fiscal years.

Currently budget projections made in budget baselines show declining deficits over the budget window. Many budget analysts agree that these projections give the misleading impression that there is not a long-term fiscal imbalance for two reasons. First, the gradual nature of the projected growth in elderly entitlement spending leads to small increases over short periods but significant increases over long periods. Second, it is argued that the baseline leads to deficit projections that are downward biased due to the way that it is calculated, as assumptions typically yield higher revenue estimates and slower growth of discretionary spending relative to current policy.

Both OMB and CBO compute baseline projections using assumptions set out in budget enforcement legislation, and this legislation requires baselines to follow current law (as opposed to current policy).[34] The legislative and macroeconomic assumptions used can greatly affect baseline estimates and projections. Specifically, CBO assumes that discretionary spending remains constant in inflation-adjusted terms, that the 2001 and 2003 tax cuts fully expire after 2010 (as current law specifies), and that one-year "patches" to the AMT will lapse. Depending on when military supplemental bills are enacted, the baseline can also sometimes partially omit those costs (because it only incorporates enacted legislation, not legislation that is likely to be enacted).[35] If the baseline concept is well understood, then these assumptions are not misleading. If the public or policymakers interpret the baseline to be a "best guess" of future outcomes, however, then the baseline would arguably give a misleadingly rosy outlook of the fiscal situation. To make the budget more transparent, Congress could consider revising the statutory assumptions required to calculate the baseline in order to gain a more realistic picture of the budget deficit.

An alternative perspective is that greater transparency is not needed because the long-term fiscal imbalance is already well known and understood by policymakers and the public. As this report has outlined, official government sources already release several detailed estimates of the longterm fiscal imbalance, the President's Fiscal Commission and several independent organizations are working on detailed proposals to rectify the imbalance, and many policymakers have highlighted the issue in various forums. In this view, the problem is not a lack of understanding but a lack of consensus as to how best solve the problem. Postponing a decision may be preferable to those directly affected since sacrifices, in the form of higher taxes or lower spending necessary to solve the problem, are likely to seem painful.

End Notes

[1] For more information on the budget process, see CRS Report 98-721, Introduction to the Federal Budget Process, coordinated by Bill Heniff Jr.

[2] For more information on the long-term budget outlook and policy options, see CRS Report RL32747, The Economic Implications of the Long-Term Federal Budget Outlook, by Marc Labonte. For more information on budget reform, see CRS Report R40113, Federal Budget Process Reform in the 111th Congress: A Brief Overview, by Megan Suzanne Lynch.

[3] OMB, Budget for Fiscal Year 2011, Analytical Perspectives, p. 45.

[4] Requirements for CBO's baseline can be found in Section 257 of the Balanced Budget and Emergency Deficit Control Act of 1985 (P.L. 99-177). The baseline is released by CBO in The Economic and Budget Outlook near the beginning of the calendar year and is updated once a year before the end of the same fiscal year.

[5] Specifically, section 301(a) of the Congressional Budget Act of 1974 (P.L. 93-344) (The Budget Act) states that the concurrent resolution shall set forth appropriate levels for the fiscal year beginning on October 1 of such year and at least four ensuing fiscal years for the following—(1) totals of new budget authority and outlays; (2) total federal revenues and the amount, if any, by which the aggregate level of federal revenues should be increases or decreased by bills and resolutions to be reported by the appropriate committees; (3) the surplus or deficit in the budget; (4) new budget authority and outlays for each major functional category, based on allocations of the total levels set forth pursuant to paragraph (1); and (5) the public debt; etc.

[6] For more information on budget resolutions, see CRS Report 98-815, Budget Resolution Enforcement, by Bill Heniff Jr. and CRS Report 98-512, Formulation and Content of the Budget Resolution, by Bill Heniff Jr.

[7] The current policy baseline was first used in President Obama's FY2010 budget.

[8] Section 402(1) of The Budget Act.

[9] For more information, see CRS Report RL32835, PAYGO Rules for Budget Enforcement in the House and Senate, by Robert Keith and Bill Heniff Jr.

[10] The Statutory Pay-As-You-Go Act of 2010 (P.L. 111-139). For more information on Statutory PAYGO, see CRS Report R41157, The Statutory Pay-As-You-Go Act of 2010: Summary and Legislative History, by Bill Heniff Jr.

[11] CBO's most recently published Long-Term Budget Outlook can be found at http://www.cbo.gov/doc.cfm?index= 11579.

[12] GAO, The Federal Government's Long-Term Fiscal Outlook, most recent from November 2010, available at http://www.gao.gov/new.items/d11201sp.pdf.

[13] The most recent report from the Social Security Trustees can be found at http://social security.gov/OACT/TR/2010/ tr2010.pdf. The most recent report from the Medicare Trustees can be found at https://www.cms.gov/ ReportsTrustFunds/ downloads/tr2010.pdf.

[14] The FY2009 report is available at http://www.fms.treas.gov/fr/09frusg/09frusg.pdf. The FY2010 report is scheduled for release in December 2010.

[15] This exists as part of the "Byrd Rule," Section 313(b) of The Budget Act.

[16] This was included in section 311(b) of the budget resolution for FY2009: S.Con.Res. 70 (110th Congress). This is scheduled to expire on September 30, 2017.

[17] Section 13302(a) Budget Enforcement Act of 1990 (P.L. 101-508).

[18] As specified in H.Res. 5 (112th Congress) Separate orders (g) Limitation on Long-term Spending.

[19] Separate from official scores, CBO has provided detailed long-term cost estimates of certain Social Security reform and healthcare legislation in the past.

[20] Unless otherwise noted, years in this report refer to the federal fiscal year. References to debt are to debt held by the public, not gross debt.

[21] Congressional Budget Office, The Long-Term Budget Outlook, June 2010, Table1-2, available at http://www.cbo.gov/doc.cfm?index=11579.

[22] Although this quote is widely used when discussing various types of budget process reform, it is typically attributed to former CBO Director Rudolph G. Penner. The first found reference is Elizabeth Wehr, "Congress Likely to Resist Budget Process Change," Congressional Quarterly Weekly Report, December 27, 1986, p. 3142.

[23] CBO, The Uncertainty of Budget Projections: A Discussion of Data and Methods, March 2007, Table 6.

[24] CBO has provided long-term estimates of the effects in the scores of certain Social Security and healthcare reform legislation in the past.

[25] Debt targets typically exclude intergovernmental debt because it is owed from one part of the government to another and is not affected by budget deficits. Therefore, debt targets are typically for publicly held debt rather than gross debt.

[26] Because the regular legislative process can be time consuming and procedurally cumbersome, expedited procedures, also referred to as "fast-track" procedures, are sometimes enacted to allow specific legislation to enjoy special procedures protecting them from many typical obstacles. Since the goal of such procedures is to ensure Congress's ability to consider the measure, and to do so in a timely manner, Congress is confirming that it deems the specified measure to be of unique importance. For more information on expedited procedures see

CRS Report RS20234, Expedited or "Fast-Track" Legislative Procedures, by Christopher M. Davis.

[27] For more information see CRS Report RL33030, The Budget Reconciliation Process: House and Senate Procedures, by Robert Keith and Bill Heniff Jr.

[28] CRS Report R40480, Budget Reconciliation Measures Enacted Into Law: 1980-2010, by Megan Suzanne Lynch.

[29] P.L. 101-508.

[30] The primary exceptions are federal loans and loan guarantees that are subject to the Federal Credit Reform Act. The estimated subsidy from these programs is recorded as an outlay in the year the loan or guarantee is made on a net present value basis.

[31] Net present value allows data to be compared over time by reducing future year data by a discount rate. Under this method, values further into the future get discounted more.

[32] Presumably, under accrual-basis accounting, the budgetary totals would reflect net expenditures, since Medicare expenditures are currently included in budgetary totals net of premiums. Alternatively, gross expenditures and gross revenues could be included in budgetary totals.

[33] Proponents may take as a given that promised benefits in elderly entitlement programs would be recognized as liabilities under an accrual accounting system. But since Treasury's accrual-based estimates do not currently do so, a switch to accrual accounting may also require a change in government accounting conventions to achieve the desired goal. For more information, see Government Accountability Office, Understanding Similarities and Differences between Accrual and Cash Deficits, GAO-07-117SP, December 2006.

[34] Both OMB and CBO generally follow the rules set forth in Section 257 of the Deficit Control Act of 1985. Although some budget enforcement legislation constraining the computation of baseline estimates has expired, CBO has indicated that it will follow these practices until directed otherwise by Congress.

[35] The OMB current services baseline arguably addresses some of these concerns.

INDEX

N

O

P